Fundamentals of
Procedure
in
Actions at Law

Fundamentals of Procedure in Actions at Law

By

Austin Wakeman Scott

Story Professor of Law in Harvard University

BeardBooks

Washington, D.C.

To my father
AUSTIN SCOTT
My first instructor in the law

PREFACE

In the following pages the author has discussed certain phases of some of the problems with which he deals in his course on Civil Procedure in the Harvard Law School. Emphasis has been laid upon the jurisdictional and constitutional aspects of the problems discussed; hence the somewhat general title of the book. Two of the chapters have in substance already appeared in the Harvard Law Review.

TABLE OF CONTENTS

TABLE OF CASES CITED

CHAPTER I

In the early days of the nineteenth century Edward Livingston of New York went to New Orleans. He there acquired an interest in an extensive tract of land upon the water-front called the Batture Ste. Marie. This land was claimed by the United States government as national property. Acting under the orders of President Jefferson, the United States marshal ejected Mr. Livingston and his employees from the tract in question. Subsequently Livingston brought an action of trespass *quare clausum fregit* in the Circuit Court of the United States for the District of Virginia, against Jefferson, who was no longer President, claiming damages in the sum of $100,000. Jefferson pleaded to the jurisdiction, alleging that the land in question was situated in the territory of Orleans outside the District of Virginia. Livingston replied that Jefferson was not a resident of Orleans and was not amenable to the jurisdiction of the courts of that territory. Jefferson demurred. It was held by the court, which was composed of Chief Justice Marshall and District Judge Tyler, that the action could not be maintained because it was based upon trespass to land situated outside the district where the action was brought.[1] Inasmuch as Jefferson was

---

1. Livingston v. Jefferson, 1 Brock. 203, Fed. Cas. No. 8411 (1811) ; SCOTT, CAS. CIV. PROC. 3.

[1]

never found in the territory of Orleans and never could be served with process there, and never owned property there which could be attached, Livingston never succeeded in maintaining an action against him. Livingston claimed that a great wrong had been committed, but he was denied the opportunity of proving it and obtaining redress. Why?

The courts have drawn a distinction between transitory and local actions, holding that the former may be brought in any jurisdiction, the latter only in a particular jurisdiction. What is the nature and what is the basis of this distinction?

It is obvious that an action to recover possession of specific land, or to affect the title thereto or some interest therein, is maintainable only in the jurisdiction in which the property involved is situated. Unless it has jurisdiction of the property, a state has no power to afford the remedy sought, and cannot confer jurisdiction upon its courts. Such proceedings, which are called proceedings *in rem,* are properly held to be local, in that they can be brought only in the particular jurisdiction where the property sought to be affected thereby is situated.[2] Relief can be given in such proceedings, however, even though the persons affected are not subject to the jurisdiction of the court. It is true that such persons are in gen-

2. See GOULD, PLEADING, ch. 3, §§ 106, 109; 40 CYC. 31, notes 96-98.

eral entitled to notice of the proceedings and an opportunity to be heard; but it is not necessary that they should be subject to the jurisdiction of the state or of the court in which the proceedings are brought.[3]

Quite different however was the problem in *Livingston* v. *Jefferson*. In that case, it is true, the plaintiff based his right of action upon an interest in land; but he sought only to obtain a judgment imposing a personal liability upon the defendant. It was a proceeding *in personam*. Why might not the court properly have given a judgment imposing such liability, since it had jurisdiction of the person of the defendant? The practical result of holding that an action to recover damages for injuries to land can be brought only in the jurisdiction where the land lies, is in many cases to deprive of all remedy a plaintiff who admittedly has been wronged. This obvious failure of justice raises a presumption against the soundness of the decision in *Livingston* v. *Jefferson*. And yet that decision represents the law in England today, and has been followed in almost all of the American states where the question has

3. The federal Judicial Code, § 57, provides for service by publication upon nonresidents in suits in a federal District Court "to enforce any legal or equitable lien upon or claim to, or to remove any incumbrance or lien or cloud upon the title to real or personal property within the district;" but as against absent defendants who do not appear the adjudication affects only the property subject to the jurisdiction of the court. See Louisville & Nashville R. R. Co. v. Western Union Tel. Co., 234 U. S. 369, 58 L. ed. 1356, 34 Sup. Ct. 810 (1914).

arisen.[4] Is there any justification for these decisions, either in logic or in policy?

It has been frequently suggested by the courts that actions should be held to be transitory when the transactions on which they are founded might have taken place anywhere; and should be held local when the transactions could not have taken place anywhere except where they did take place. No one however has ever suggested any reason why it should make any difference whether events might or might not have occurred at some other place than where they did occur. Moreover, since every event is the result of an infinite train of causes, it may be said that nothing could have happened at any other place or in any other way than where and as it did happen. Surely one who believes in the doctrine of fore-ordination would take this view. Or it might be said that if there had been some change in the line of causation everything might have happened differently from the way in which it did happen. If geological conditions had been different or if our colonial history had been different, land in New York might have been situated in Massachusetts. It would seem difficult to support the distinction between

4. See cases cited, WHARTON, CONFLICT OF LAWS (3 ed.), §§ 290, 290a; SCOTT, CAS. CIV. PROC. 8; 26 L. R. A. (N. S.) 935; 3 ANN. CAS. 344; 40 CYC. 31.

If an act is done in one state causing injury to land in another, it is generally held that an action may be maintained in the former state as well as in the latter. Smith v. Southern Ry. Co., 136 Ky. 162, 123 S. W. 678, 26 L. R. A. (N. S.) 927 (1909).

local and transitory actions upon such metaphysical speculations.

The statement that a cause of action is local when it could have arisen only in a particular place, and is transitory when it might have arisen anywhere, being valueless as a reason for the distinction between local and transitory actions, is of possible interest only as a crude attempt to state the nature of that distinction. What is meant is that if a cause of action is founded upon a thing which is immovable, which usually means land, the action is local. Thus the following actions, as well as proceedings *in rem* and actions to recover damages for trespass upon or injury to land, have been held to be local: replevin at common law;[5] actions upon covenants running with the land when based upon privity of estate;[6]

---

5. Actions of replevin at common law were held to be local, and maintainable only where the cause of action arose. At common law, it is to be remembered, replevin lay only for wrongful distress. The owner of land might distrain for rent in arrear or he might distrain cattle doing damage upon his land. If the owner of the property distrained brought replevin therefor, the venue had to be laid where the land was situated for which rent was alleged to be due or upon which the damage was alleged to have taken place. Today replevin can usually be brought wherever the property is found, or in some jurisdictions wherever it has been detained; and need not be brought where the cause of action arose. Central Maine Power Co. v. Maine Central R. R. Co., 113 Me. 103, 93 Atl. 41 (1915); Stuart v. Baldwin, 41 U. C. Q. B. 446, 479 (1877). In most states the action is not a proceeding *in rem*, for if the property is not found by the sheriff the plaintiff may recover its value in damages.

6. When an action upon a covenant running with land is brought by the original covenantee against the original covenantor, an action of debt for arrears of a rent-charge when based upon privity of estate;[7] an action against an innkeeper based upon the custom of the realm.[8] These actions are all in some manner connected with land. But why should they be held to be local?

It has been suggested that as a practical matter it is more difficult to determine questions relating to title to land situated in another jurisdiction than it is to ascertain the truth as to other matters occurring in another jurisdiction. Even if this is true, and its truth may well be doubted, it proves too much. In the first place, an action to recover damages for trespass to land is held to be local although there is no dispute as to the title to the land. The action cannot be maintained even though the plaintiff's title is admitted, and the real dispute for instance is whether or not the plaintiff had given the defendant permission to enter. A declaration stating as a cause of action trespass to land outside the jurisdiction is held to be bad on its face and therefore demurrable.

it is said to be based upon "privity of contract," and, like other actions upon contracts, is transitory. Phelps v. Decker, 10 Mass. 267 (1813); Jackson v. Hanna, 53 N. C. 188 (1860). But when the action is brought by an assignee of the covenantee or against an assignee of the covenantor, it is said to be based upon "privity of estate," and is held to be local. Clark v. Scudder, 6 Gray (Mass.) 122 (1856); White v. Sanborn, 6 N. H. 220 (1833); GOULD, PLEADING, ch. 3, §§ 116-124; 26 L. R. A. (N. S.) 928.

7. Whitaker v. Forbes, 1 C. P. D. 51 (C. A., 1875).

8. Anon., Godb. 42 (1587).

So also an action for wilfully or negligently causing injury to the plaintiff's land is demurrable.[9]
In the second place, an action for breach of contract[10] or for injury to the person or to personal
property, is held to be transitory even though title
to land is put in issue.[11]

In *Livingston* v. *Jefferson*, Chief Justice Marshall said:

9. In a few cases it has been held that where the injury to
land is a result of negligence and the action is in the nature of
a common-law action of case as distinguished from trespass, the
action is transitory. This distinction however has generally been
rejected. Karr v. New York Jewell Co., 78 N. J. L. 198, 73
Atl. 132 (1909); Brisbane v. Pa. R. R. Co., 205 N. Y. 431
(1912); Brereton v. Canadian Pac. Ry. Co., 29 Ont. Rep. 57
(1897).

10. Unless based upon privity of estate. See note 6, *supra*.

11. See Stone v. United States, 167 U. S. 178, 42 L. ed. 127,
17 Sup. Ct. 778 (1897) (conversion of timber); Hodges v. Hunter
Co., 61 Fla. 280, 54 So. 811 (1911) (conversion of timber);
McGonigle v. Atchison, 33 Kans. 726, 7 Pac. 550 (1885) (conversion of sand); Brady v. Brady, 161 N. C. 324, 77 S. E. 235
(1913) (proceeds of the sale of timber wrongfully cut).

An action for use and occupation will lie in one state against
one in possession of the plaintiff's land situated in another state.
Henwood v. Cheeseman, 3 Serg. & R. (Pa.) 500 (1817); Shep-
pard v. Coeur d'Alene Lumber Co., 62 Wash. 12, 112 Pac. 932,
44 L. R. A. (N. S.) 267 (1911). See GOULD, PLEADING, ch. 3,
§ 125.

So also an action may be maintained by a lessor against the
lessee for waste although the land is situated outside the state.
Campbell v. W. M. Ritter Lumber Co., 140 Ky. 312, 131 S. W.
20 (1910).

So also an action for slander of title to land is transitory.
Dodge v. Colby, 108 N. Y. 445, 13 N. E. 703 (1888).

For cases in regard to suits in equity affecting land in another state, see 69 L. R. A. 672; 23 L. R. A. (N. S.) 924.

"It is admitted that on a contract respecting lands, an action is sustainable wherever the defendant may be found. Yet in such a case every difficulty may occur that presents itself in an action of trespass. An investigation of title may become necessary, a question of boundary may arise, and a survey may be essential to the full merits of the cause. Yet these difficulties have not prevailed against the jurisdiction of the court. They are countervailed, and more than countervailed, by the opposing consideration that if the action be disallowed, the injured party may have a clear right without a remedy, in a case where a person who has done the wrong, and who ought to make the compensation, is within the power of the court."

In *Stone* v. *United States*,[12] an action was brought by the United States in the District Court of the United States for the District of Washington to recover the value of certain timber and railroad ties manufactured from trees alleged to have been unlawfully cut by the defendant from certain lands in Idaho of which the plaintiff alleged that it was owner. The defendant interposed a general denial. It was held that the action could be maintained. The court said:

"In the present case the petition, it is true, avers that the United States was the owner

12. 167 U. S. 178, 42 L. ed. 127, 17 Sup. Ct. 778 (1897).

of the lands from which the trees were cut, but the gravamen of the action was the conversion of the lumber and the railroad ties manufactured out of such trees, and a judgment was asked, not for the trespass, but for the value of the personal property so converted by the defendant. The description in the petition of the lands and the averment of ownership in the United States were intended to show the right of the government to claim the value of the personal property manufactured from the trees illegally taken from its lands. Although the [defendant's] denial of the ownership of the land made it necessary for [the plaintiff] to prove its ownership, the action in its essential features related to personal property, was of a transitory nature, and could be brought in any jurisdiction in which the defendant could be found and served with process.''

The court, it is true, had no jurisdiction to determine the title to the land in question, except incidentally for the purpose of determining whether there had been a conversion of personalty. Its decision would not render the question as to title *res judicata;* for the jurisdiction finally to determine a controversy as to title to land rests only with the courts of the state where the land is situated. But the court did have jurisdiction to determine whether there had been a conversion of the timber, and incidentally for that purpose to determine the question of title to the land.[13] It is difficult to see why the court should not also have jurisdiction to determine whether the plaintiff is entitled to recover damages for trespass to the land, even though incidentally a question of title to land is involved.

13. See Stuart v. Baldwin, 41 U. C. Q. B. 446, 479 (1877).

In a recent Massachusetts case in which the plaintiff brought an action for conversion of ore alleged to have been wrongfully dug in Arizona, where there was a *bona fide* dispute as to the title to the land from which the ore was taken, both parties being corporations organized under the laws of Maine, the court held that the action should be dismissed. Arizona Mining Co. v. Iron Cap Copper Co., 236 Mass. 185, 128 N. E. 4 (1920). An action had been brought in Maine between the same parties and based upon the same transaction, in which the plaintiff was allowed to recover (119 Me. 213, 110 Atl. 429 [1920]); but the Massachusetts court distinguished this case on the ground that both parties were Maine corporations. In most jurisdictions the place of residence of the parties is immaterial. In a few states however the courts have declined to exercise jurisdiction in controversies between nonresidents arising outside the state, although the cause of action is in its nature transitory. See Matthaei v. Galitzin, L. R. 18 Eq. 340 (1874); Gardner v. Thomas, 14 Johns. (N. Y.) 134 (1817). See NEW YORK CORPORATION LAW, §§ 46, 47. In Massachusetts however it has been held that in transitory actions the fact that both parties are nonresidents is immaterial. Peabody v. Hamilton, 106 Mass. 217 (1870).

In some jurisdictions it is held that even though the land is situated within the jurisdiction, an action of assumpsit for the proceeds of property severed from the land will not lie if the defendant was in adverse possession of the land under claim of title. Parks v. Morris, Layfield & Co., 63 W. Va. 51, 59 S. E. 753 (1907). See 89 AM. DEC. 427. And in some states the same rule has been adopted as to actions of trover and replevin. See 89 AM. DEC. 429. Under this rule *a fortiori* such actions cannot be maintained outside of the state where the land is situated. See Arizona Mining Co. v. Iron Cap Copper Co., *supra;*

Suppose that the plaintiff alleges in a single count that the defendant wrongfully entered upon the plaintiff's land outside the state and removed personal property therefrom. Is his declaration or complaint demurrable? In jurisdictions in which the common-law forms of action are retained, the plaintiff suing in one form of action, *e.g.* trespass *quare clausum fregit,* cannot recover on any cause of action for which a different form of action is required, *e. g.* trover for conversion of personalty. But how is it in jurisdictions in which forms of action have been abolished?

In *Ellenwood* v. *Marietta Chair Company,*[14] the plaintiff brought an action in the Circuit Court of the United States for the Southern District of Ohio, alleging in his complaint that he was the owner and in possession of certain land in West Virginia and of the timber growing thereon, and that on January 1, 1875, and divers other days from time to time continuously between that day and May 4, 1885, the defendant cut down and removed and sawed into logs a large quantity of the timber and converted the logs to its own use. It was held that the action could not be maintained. The court said:

> "This allegation was of a single cause of action, in which the trespass upon the land was the principal thing, and the conversion

Ophir Silver Min. Co. v. Superior Court, 147 Calif. 467, 82 **Pac.** 70 (1905).

14. 158 U. S. 105, 39 L. ed. 913, 15 Sup. Ct. 771 (1895).

of the timber was incidental only; and could not, therefore, be maintained by proof of the conversion of personal property, without also proving the trespass upon real estate. [Cases cited.] The entire cause of action was local. The land alleged to have been trespassed upon being in West Virginia, the action could not be maintained in Ohio."

A similar result has been reached in other cases.[15]

In Wisconsin, however, the opposite result has been reached. In *Bruheim* v. *Stratton*,[16] the plaintiff brought an action in Wisconsin, alleging that he was the owner of certain lands in Minnesota, and that between November, 1903, and March, 1904, the defendant wrongfully entered upon this land and cut timber growing thereon and took and carried the same away and converted the same to his own use. The trial court held that the court had no jurisdiction. It was held by the Supreme Court that this ruling was erroneous. The court said:

15. Dodge v. Colby, 108 N. Y. 445, 13 N. E. 703 (1888); Montesano Lumber Co. v. Portland Iron Works, 78 Ore. 53, 152 Pac. 244 (1915); Brereton v. Can. Pac. Ry. Co., 29 Ont. Rep. 57 (1897).

In Jacobus v. Colgate, 217 N. Y. 235, 111 N. E. 837 (1916), it was held that the complaint stated two causes of action, one for injury to land, the other for injury to personalty, and that although the court had jurisdiction of the action for injury to personalty, the whole complaint was demurrable for misjoinder of causes of action. *Sed quaere.*

16. 145 Wis. 271, 129 N. W. 1092 (1911); SCOTT, CAS. CIV. PROC. 105.

"There were sufficient allegations in the complaint to make a good cause of action in conversion, and what the idea of the pleader was when he drew the complaint was immaterial. If the allegations were sufficient to constitute a cause of action in conversion the plaintiff was entitled to have it treated as such by the court, and the fact that the court had no jurisdiction of the action of trespass upon the land in another state rendered the allegations respecting a cause of action in trespass merely surplusage, and, there being sufficient allegations aside from these to make the complaint one in conversion, it should have been so treated by the court. [Cases cited.] Doubtless the complaint as originally drawn would have been subject to a motion to make more definite and certain or to strike out the surplus allegations, but no such motion was made and defendant answered on the merits."

This decision seems preferable to that in *Ellenwood* v. *Marietta Chair Company*. If the plaintiff states sufficient facts to constitute a cause of action on any theory, the action should not be dismissed merely because it could not be maintained upon the theory upon which the court thinks the plaintiff intended to rely.[17]

17. See 33 HARV. L. REV. 240-242.

If there is a s'ngle inseverable cause of action, and if the plaintiff is allowed to recover for the injury to personalty, he

It would seem on principle that proceedings *in personam,* including actions to recover damages for trespass to land, should be held to be transitory. This was the view of Lord Mansfield expressed in two unreported cases at *nisi prius,* and by way of dictum in the case of *Mostyn v. Fabrigas,*[18] decided by the King's Bench. But this view unfortunately was repudiated by the English courts.[19] When the question whether an action to recover a judgment for damages for trespass to land is local or transitory first came up in the United States in the case of *Livingston* v. *Jefferson,* the injustice of holding such an action to be local was strongly pressed upon the court. By no one has the injustice of such a holding been more clearly presented than by Chief Justice Marshall in his opinion. He approved of

cannot later recover for the injury to the land. 2 BLACK, JUDGMENTS (2 ed.), § 734.

18. ''There is a formal and a substantial distinction as to the locality of trials. I state them as different things; the substantial distinction is, where the proceeding is *in rem,* and where the effect of the judgment cannot be had, if it is laid in a wrong place. That is the case of all ejectments, where possession is to be delivered by the sheriff of the county; and as trials in England are in particular counties, the officers are county officers; therefore the judgment could not have effect, if the action was not laid in the proper county. . . . So if an action were brought relative to an estate in a foreign country, where the question was a matter of title only, and not of damages, there might be a solid distinction of locality.'' Mostyn v. Fabrigas, 1 Cowp. 161, 176 (1774).

19. Doulson v. Matthews, 4 T. R. 503 (1792). See also Skinner v. East India Co., 6 State Trials 710 (1666); Shelling v. Farmer, 1 Str. 646 (1725).

the distinction drawn by Lord Mansfield but felt precluded by the English decisions from applying it. He said:

> "I have not yet discerned a reason, other than a technical one, which can satisfy my judgment. If, however, this technical reason is firmly established, if all other judges respect it, I cannot venture to disregard it."

It is interesting to remember that there existed between Jefferson and Marshall political enmity and personal animosity, and that Jefferson's private fortune was at stake in this litigation. It would have been very difficult undoubtedly for Marshall to depart from the English precedents when to do so would have involved a serious loss to Jefferson. Possibly therefore he leaned backward.[20] Judge Tyler, on the other hand, enthusiastically concurred with the English precedents. Indeed the only excuse for some of his language [21] would seem to be found in the statement at the end of his opinion that he was unwell at the time he gave it.

In almost every state in which the question has arisen, the courts, though frequently expressing dissatisfaction on principle with the result reached in *Livingston* v. *Jefferson,* have never-

20. See 4 BEVERIDGE, LIFE OF MARSHALL, 100; HUNT, LIFE OF LIVINGSTON, chap. 8.

21. "It is the happy talent of some professional gentlemen, and particularly of the plaintiff's counsel, often to make 'the worse appear the better cause.'"

theless felt bound to follow that decision. Minnesota is a notable exception. In *Little* v. *Chicago, St. Paul, Minneapolis & Omaha Railway Company,*[22] the plaintiff brought an action in Minnesota alleging that the defendant railway company had by its negligence started a fire which injured the plaintiff's land in Wisconsin. The defendant answered, *inter alia,* that the court had no jurisdiction of the cause of action. The trial court overruled a demurrer to the answer. On appeal the Supreme Court held that the order overruling the demurrer was erroneous. A majority of the justices were of the opinion that the rule that an action cannot be maintained for injury to land outside the jurisdiction is unsound on principle, that this rule had not been definitely adopted in England prior to the American Revolution, and that the doctrine of *stare decisis* did not require the American courts to adopt it. Mitchell, J., one of the ablest judges who has sat upon the Supreme Court of Minnesota, speaking for the majority, said:

"Almost every court or judge who has ever discussed the question has criticised or condemned the rule as technical, wrong on principle, and often resulting in a total denial of justice, and yet has considered himself bound to adhere to it under the doctrine of *stare decisis.* . . .

"We recognize the respect due to judicial

22. 65 Minn. 48, 67 N. W. 846 (1896).

precedents, and the authority of the doctrine of *stare decisis;* but, inasmuch as this rule is in no sense a rule of property, and as it is purely technical, wrong in principle, and in practice often results in a total denial of justice, and has been so generally criticised by eminent jurists, we do not feel bound to adhere to it, notwithstanding the great array of judicial decisions in its favor. If the courts of England, generations ago, were at liberty to invent a fiction in order to change the ancient rule that all actions were local, and then fix their own limitations to the application of the fiction, we cannot see why the courts of the present day should deem themselves slavishly bound by those limitations.''[23]

In Louisiana, where the common law is not in force, an action to recover damages for trespass to land outside the state, is maintainable.[24]

From the foregoing discussion and from the dissatisfaction so frequently expressed in the cases, it would seem that there is no justification based either on logic or on policy for the rule that an action cannot be maintained to recover damages for trespass to land outside the jurisdiction. On the contrary the rule, it is submitted, is unsound in principle and frequently results in a

23. The federal courts situated in Minnesota have followed the Minnesota rule. See Peyton v. Desmond, 129 Fed. 1, 63 C. C. A. 651 (1904).

24. Holmes v. Barclay, 4 La. Ann. 63 (1849).

denial of justice.[25] The existence of the rule can be explained, however, as a matter of history.

In the early days of our common-law procedure, the jurors decided issues not merely in accordance with the evidence offered at the trial, but in part at least upon their own knowledge of the facts involved. Naturally therefore it was necessary that the jurors should come not merely from the county but from the immediate vicinity, the parish, town or hamlet, in which the facts in controversy took place; for otherwise presumably they would not be cognizant of those facts. Every fact relied upon in the pleadings had to be stated as having occurred at a certain place. It was the place at which the facts in issue were asserted to have occurred that determined the venue, the place from which the jurors should be selected. The venue therefore did not depend upon the place where the cause of action arose, unless the defendant denied the facts constituting the cause of action. At first the jurors were summoned to Westminster, where they took part in the trial held at the bar of the court. When the *nisi prius* system was introduced in the thirteenth century, actions came to be tried as a rule in the various counties before the judges on circuit. Nevertheless the function of the jurors was the same, namely to determine the issues upon their own knowledge as well as upon

25. See Kuhn, ''Local and Transitory Actions in Private International Law,'' 66 U. PA. L. REV. 301 (1918); Storke, "The Venue of Actions of Trespass to Land," 27 W. VA. L. QUAR. 301 (1921). See also 22 ALB. L. J. 47; 40 CYC. 18.

the evidence presented in court. It was still necessary that the jurors should be selected from the place where the facts in issue occurred.

Gradually however as the centuries drifted by, the functions of jurors and witnesses were becoming differentiated. The jurors were becoming more and more judges upon evidence given before them by witnesses, and less and less recognitors acting on their own knowledge of the facts. The reason for requiring the issues to be tried by a jury of the vicinage ceased, and gradually the rules as to venue were relaxed. In 1585 for instance a statute [26] provided that it should be sufficient if two of the jurors came from the hundred where the facts in issue occurred; they could inform their fellows as to what they knew of those facts. In 1705 a statute [27] provided that it was sufficient if the jurors came from the body of the county in which the issue was triable.

At the same time the law as to the manner of laying the venue was undergoing a change. The plaintiff would state in the margin of the declaration the name of the county where the cause of action or some part of it arose; *e.g.* "Middlesex, to wit." This was called the venue in the action, as distinguished from the fact-venue, *i.e.* the venue laid for each fact stated in the body of the pleadings. By statute[28] in 1664 it was provided that

26. STAT. 27 ELIZ. c. 6, § 5.
27. STAT. 4 ANNE c. 16, § 6.
28. STAT. 17 CAR. II c. 8.

judgment after verdict should not be stayed or
reversed on account of the venue if the cause were
tried by a jury of the proper county where the action was laid. It came to be the practice thereafter that the place from which the jury should be
selected was determined by the venue laid in the
margin of the declaration, and not by the venue
stated in the body of the pleadings. The laying
of a venue in the body of the pleadings became a
mere matter of form,[29] and finally in 1834 it was
provided in the Hilary Rules [30] that the name of
a county should be stated in the margin of the
declaration, and should be taken to be the venue
intended by the plaintiff, and that no venue should
be stated in the body of the declaration or in any
subsequent pleading, although in cases where a
local description was required such local description should be given.[31]

How far was it necessary that the venue should
be laid truly? When the jurors were selected because of their knowledge of the facts in issue it
was clearly necessary in all cases to state the
venue truly. But as the functions of jurors and
witnesses became differentiated, it became unim-
portant to select the jury from any particular
locality. Hence if the place in which the cause of
action arose was not a material part of the description of the cause of action, the plaintiff might

29. Ilderton v. Ilderton, 2 H. Bl. 145 (1793). See GOULD,
PLEADING, ch. 3, §§ 132-165.

30. REG. GEN. HIL. T. 4 WILL. IV, reg. 8.

31. See STEPHEN, PLEADING, *315-*323.

allege in his declaration that the facts constituting his cause of action arose in one place although in fact they arose in another place. The allegation as to the place, not being a material allegation, could not be traversed by the defendant; if the place proved at the trial was different from that laid in the declaration, the plaintiff could not be nonsuited for a variance. Thus in an action for battery alleged to have been committed in Middlesex, the plaintiff would win if he proved that the battery was committed, although committed in Surrey or even outside the realm.[32]

In some cases however the place might be a material part of the description of the cause of action, as in the case of an action on a covenant which showed on its face where it was executed. In such cases unless the plaintiff stated the place truly he would be guilty of a variance. In such cases the plaintiff was allowed to state the true place, and then lay the venue under a *videlicet;* e.g. "at Amsterdam, to wit in the county of Middlesex." So also in an action for the seizure of a ship it might be necessary to state that the seizure occurred on the high seas, but the plaintiff might add "to wit in London in the ward of Cheap." The defendant was not allowed to traverse these allegations. Thus actions might be tried in any county in England, although they arose in a different county or outside the realm.[33]

32. Mostyn v. Fabrigas, Cowp. 161, 176 (1774).

33. See Mostyn v. Fabrigas, Cowp. 161, 177 (1774), and cases cited; GOULD, PLEADING, ch. 3, § 160.

The courts might well have applied these convenient fictions in all cases of actions *in personam*. Lord Mansfield, as has been stated, saw no objection to allowing an action to be brought in England to recover damages for trespass to land outside England. All that was necessary was, he thought, after stating where the land was really situated, to lay the venue under a *videlicet* in an English county. But to state, even under a *videlicet,* that land was in any place except where it really was, involved too much of a stretch of the imagination for the other English judges. They could swallow the fiction that a covenant executed in the East Indies was executed in Middlesex, or that a ship on the high seas was in Cheapside, but not that land situated in Canada was situated anywhere in England, or that land situated in one English county was situated in another English county.[34] Hence arose the distinction between transitory and local actions.[35]

As long as the cause of action arose somewhere in England the only question was one of the place of trial. An action in any of His Majesty's superior courts would be brought at Westminster, and a writ might be served upon the defendant in any county in which he could be found, and the judgment against him rendered by the court at Westminster might be enforced in any county in which he might have property. But to hold that

[34]. Shelling v. Farmer, 1 Str. 646 (1725); Doulson v. Matthews, 4 T. R. 503 (1792).

[35]. STEPHEN, PLEADING, *323-*328; 40 CYC. 17.

an action to recover damages for trespass to land outside of England could not be tried in any English county and could not therefore be maintained anywhere in England, was a very serious matter. The plaintiff was often left without a remedy, for no action could be maintained in the jurisdiction where the land lay unless the plaintiff was fortunate enough to find the defendant or his property there. It is still more serious, especially in these days of constant and close intercommunication, to hold that an action for trespass to land in one American state cannot be maintained in another.[36] In those states, fortunately few in number,[37] in which the process of the courts does not run throughout the state, but only in the county in which the action is brought, the result is still more unfortunate; for in such states it is possible for the defendant to escape liability by remaining and keeping his property outside the county in which the land is situated, even though he or his property may be found in some other county of the same state.[38]

36. A possible remedy has been suggested by Professor Walter Wheeler Cook. He suggests that Congress might constitutionally provide for the service and execution throughout the United States of the judicial process of the several states. See Cook, "The Powers of Congress under the Full Faith and Credit Clause," 28 YALE L. JOUR. 421 (1919).

37. See 19 ENCYC. PL. & PR. 604.

38. For this reason it has been held in Ohio that an action upon a covenant running with land situated in a different county from that in which the action is brought, is transitory, though based upon privity of estate. Genin v. Grier, 10 Oh. 209 (1840).

Unfortunately Congress has treated the federal judicial districts not as counties of the same state but as separate states are treated. If an action is brought in a federal District Court, process cannot be served upon the defendant in any federal district not situated in the same state.[39] Hence in the case of local actions the defendant by keeping out of the state in which the cause of action arose, may avoid being sued in any federal court. This is indeed exactly what happened in *Livingston* v. *Jefferson*. The difficulty would have been avoided if Congress had provided that process issuing out of a federal court might be served in any part of the United States.

If an action is brought to recover damages for trespass to land outside the state, is the objection jurisdictional? "Jurisdiction is the power to adjudicate a case upon the merits and dispose of it as justice may require."[40] "Jurisdiction controls the judicial capacity to hear the case; venue answers only the question of where the case should be heard."[41]

It is clear that if a court has no jurisdiction of the cause of action, or, in proceedings *in rem*, of the subject of the action,[42] the defect is not waived

39. JUDICIAL CODE, § 54.

40. The Resolute, 168 U. S. 437, 42 L. ed. 533, 18 Sup. Ct. 112 (1897), *per* Brown, J.

41. See Dobie, "Venue in the United States District Court," 2 Va. L. Rev. 1 (1914).

42. Dudley v. Mayhew, 3 N. Y. 9 (1849); Wheelock v. Lee, 74 N. Y. 495 (1878); SCOTT, CAS. CIV. PROC. 71. See Two Hun-

by a plea to the merits, for such jurisdiction cannot be conferred even by the express consent of
the parties. On the other hand it is universally held
that statutes providing that actions which were
transitory at common law shall be brought only
where one of the parties resides, do not limit the
jurisdiction of the courts but merely confer a personal privilege upon the defendant, and that the
objection that the action is brought where no one
of the parties resides is waived if the defendant
pleads to the merits.[43] By the weight of authority
it is held that if an action is brought in one state
to recover damages for trespass to land situated
in another state, the objection is not merely a personal privilege of the defendant, but the court has
no jurisdiction over the cause of action.

In the case of *Ellenwood* v. *Marietta Chair Company*,[44] already referred to, an action was brought
in the Circuit Court of the United States for the
Southern District of Ohio for trespass to the land
of the plaintiff in West Virginia. The defendant
filed an answer denying the allegations in the
plaintiff's petition. It was held on writ of error
that the action was a local action, and could not
be maintained although the defendant did not by
demurrer or answer urge this objection; that the

dred Thousand Feet of Logs v. Sias, 43 Mich. 356, 5 N. W. 414
(1880).

43. Interior Construction Co. v. Gibney, 160 U. S. 217, 40 L. ed.
401, 16 Sup. Ct. 272 (1895); SCOTT, CAS. CIV. PROC. 69; McMinn
v. Hamilton, 77 N. C. 300 (1877); SCOTT, CAS. CIV. PROC. 68.

44. 158 U. S. 105, 39 L. ed. 913, 15 Sup. Ct. 771 (1895).

court had no jurisdiction of the cause of action, and that the want of jurisdiction could not be waived by the defendant's failure to object.[45] On the other hand in *Sentenis* v. *Ladew*,[46] the plaintiff brought an action in New York for trespass upon real estate in Tennessee. The defendant inter-

45. Montesano Lumber Co. v. Portland Iron Works, 78 Ore. 53, 152 Pac. 244 (1915), *accord*. See Hill v. Nelson, 70 N. J. L. 376, 57 Atl. 411 (1904).

In Allin v. Conn. River Lumber Co., 150 Mass. 560, 23 N. E. 581 (1890), it was held that a plea alleging that the land was outside the state was not a plea in abatement but showed a want of jurisdiction, and that the decision of the trial court thereon was subject to appeal. The court said: ''The objection is not that an action of which the court has jurisdiction is brought in the wrong county, but that the court has not jurisdiction of the cause of action.''

If in a local action arising within the jurisdiction, the venue is laid in the wrong county, the defect is not one of jurisdiction. Hence by consent of the parties a local action may be tried in any county. CHITTY, PLEADING (16 Am. ed.), *281. Or the court may for cause order the venue changed to any county. *Ibid.* *291.

It has been held in a number of cases that the objection that a local action is brought in the wrong county is waived by the defendant if he pleads to the merits. Gillen v. Ill. Cent. Ry. Co., 137 Ky. 375, 125 S. W. 1047 (1910); Blackford v. Lehigh Valley R. R. Co., 53 N. J. L. 56, 20 Atl. 735 (1890). *Cf.* Fletcher v. Stowell, 17 Colo. 94, 28 Pac. 326 (1891). But see *contra*, Fritts v. Camp, 94 Calif. 393, 29 Pac. 867 (1892); Central Maine Power Co. v. Maine Cent. R. R. Co., 113 Me. 103, 93 Atl. 41 (1915).

In a number of states if a local action is brought in the wrong county, the defendant may not insist upon having the action dismissed, but may have it transferred to the proper county. See Pound, ''Some Principles of Procedural Reform,'' 4 ILL. L. REV. 497.

46. 140 N. Y. 463, 35 N. E. 650 (1893).

posed an affirmative defence. The plaintiff defaulted at the trial and judgment was given against him for costs. The plaintiff later moved to set the judgment aside on the ground that the court had no jurisdiction of the subject-matter of the action and could not enter a valid judgment. It was admitted that when an action is brought for trespass to land in another jurisdiction the defendant may have the action dismissed; but it was held that the defect is not one of jurisdiction, and that the failure of the defendant to object is a waiver of his right to object. The court said:

> "If the court acquires jurisdiction of the persons of the parties by due personal service of process, or by their voluntary appearance and submission to its jurisdiction, and the defendant makes no objection to the authority of the court to hear the cause, and the parties proceed to a trial upon the merits, the judgment rendered would be neither void nor voidable for want of jurisdiction, but would be binding and conclusive upon the parties."

This reasoning has, however, been disapproved in the recent case of *Jacobus* v. *Colgate*,[47] in which Cardozo, J., referring to *Sentenis* v. *Ladew,* said that "all that was there determined was the power, where other jurisdiction fails, to award judgment for the costs." It is submitted, however, that the

47. 217 N. Y. 235, 111 N. E. 837 (1916).

reasoning of the court in *Sentenis* v. *Ladew* is sound. It is bad enough to hold as in *Livingston* v. *Jefferson* that the defendant may by timely objection prevent the rendition of a judgment against him for damages for trespass to land outside the jurisdiction; but to hold that the defect cannot be waived by the defendant is worse.

By rule of court in England it is provided that

> "There shall be no local venue for the trial of any action, except where otherwise provided by statute, but in every action in every Division the place of trial shall be fixed by the Court or a judge."[48]

In spite of this provision the House of Lords in the well-known case of *British South Africa Company v. Companhia de Moçambique*,[49] held that no action could be maintained in England to recover damages for trespass to the plaintiff's land in South Africa. Lord Herschell, L. C., said:

> "My Lords, I cannot but lay great stress upon the fact that whilst lawyers made an exception from the ordinary rule in the case of a local matter occurring outside the realm for which there was no proper place of trial in this country, and invented a fiction which enabled the Courts to exercise jurisdiction, they did not make an exception where the cause of action was a local matter arising

48. R. S. C. (1883), Order 36, rule 1, now rule 10
49. [1893] A. C. 602.

abroad, and did not extend the fiction to such cases. The rule that in local actions the venue must be local did not, where the cause of action arose in this country, touch the jurisdiction of the Courts, but only determined the particular manner in which the jurisdiction should be exercised; but where the matter complained of was local and arose outside the realm, the refusal to adjudicate upon it was in fact a refusal to exercise jurisdiction, and I cannot think that the Courts would have failed to find a remedy if they had regarded the matter as one within their jurisdiction, and which it was proper for them to adjudicate upon.''[50]

In New York in 1913 the Code of Civil Procedure was amended by a statute providing as follows:

"An action may be maintained in the courts of this state to recover damages for injuries to real estate situate without the state, or for breach of contracts or of covenants relating thereto, whenever such an action could be maintained in relation to personal property without the state.''[51]

Soon afterward the question arose whether this

---

50. See Allin v. Conn. River Lumber Co., 150 Mass. 560, 23 N. E. 581 (1890). But see Coleman v. Lucksinger, 224 Mo. 1, 123 S. W. 441 (1909), and Tillotson v. Prichard, 60 Vt. 94, 14 Atl. 302 (1887), as to actions upon covenants running with the land.

51. CODE CIV. PROC. § 982a. This section is now transferred to the Real Property Law, § 536.

statute is applicable to causes of action arising prior to its enactment. In the case of *Jacobus* v. *Colgate*,[52] this question was answered in the negative. So far as the decision involves an interpretation of the intention of the legislature, it is perhaps correct. The court took occasion however to discuss the character of the objection to the maintenance of the action at common law, and said that the defect was one of jurisdiction. Cardozo, J., said:

> "The first question to be determined is whether the courts of New York have jurisdiction of the action. . . . There is no doubt that until 1913 our courts had no jurisdiction of actions for injuries to real property lying without the state. . . . The destruction of every remedy destroys the cause of action. By parity of reasoning, the grant of a remedy where none of any kind was available, is equivalent in substance to the creation of a cause of action. We do not say that statutes of the latter class are unconstitutional because retroactive. To discuss the limits of constitutional power in that regard would lead us far afield. What we emphasize now is the distinction between statutes which merely change the procedure for the enforcement of a right and statutes which supply a remedy by which a right for the first time becomes enforceable."

52. 217 N. Y. 235, 111 N. E. 837 (1916).

Summary. It would seem on principle that the natural distinction is between proceedings *in rem* and proceedings *in personam;* that proceedings *in rem* should be, and under well-settled principles of the conflict of laws, must be local, but that proceedings *in personam* should be transitory. In other words, the character of the remedy sought, rather than the character of the plaintiff's rights, should determine whether an action is local or transitory. If the action is one in which the remedy sought is to affect property only, jurisdiction of the property is necessary, but not jurisdiction of the person of the defendant. On the other hand, if the remedy sought is the imposition of a personal obligation upon the defendant, jurisdiction of his person is necessary, but not jurisdiction of the property with respect to which the cause of action arose.

But the courts of England and of almost every American state in which the question has arisen have held that an action to recover damages for trespass upon or injury to land is local, although the proceeding is *in personam,* although the only relief sought is a judgment against the defendant for damages. Such a rule deprives the plaintiff of any remedy anywhere except where the land is situated, and he can have no relief even there unless the courts there happen to acquire jurisdiction of the defendant's person or of some property of the defendant which might be attached. The courts have usually felt the injustice of this, but have felt bound by the doctrine of *stare decisis* to follow the rule until it is changed by statute.

The rule rests upon no living principle of logic or policy, but upon a historical accident. It had its origin in a real policy which required that jurors should have personal knowledge of the facts in issue; but this policy has long been abandoned, and by the generous use of fictions the courts gradually came to hold that actions "which might have arisen anywhere" might be tried in any place which the plaintiff might select; but as a result of an innate conservatism with respect to matters affecting land, the courts refused to employ these fictions when the cause of action arose out of trespass to land, and could have arisen only where the land lies.

When a local cause of action arises within the jurisdiction, and the question is only one of the proper county, it is held that the question is one of venue, and not of the jurisdiction of the court. When however the local cause of action arises outside the jurisdiction, the courts have usually held that the question is one of jurisdiction. It is clear that the state has power to afford the relief sought when, though the action is local, the proceeding is *in personam;* but it has usually been held that in the absence of a statute conferring it the courts do not have jurisdiction of the cause of action. It has been held therefore that the defect is one which cannot be waived by the defendant, that a statute changing the rule as to venue of actions is not applicable to local causes of action arising outside the jurisdiction, and that a statute changing the rule as to local causes of action arising outside the state is not retroactive.

CHAPTER II

JURISDICTION OVER NONRESIDENTS

A personal judgment against a defendant over whom the court rendering it has no jurisdiction is invalid. It is not merely reversible on writ of error or appeal, but is void for all purposes.[1] An attempt to execute it is without justification; a sheriff levying upon property of the defendant is liable for conversion,[2] and a purchaser of the property on execution sale gets no title to it.[3] A court of equity may, where the remedy at law is inadequate, enjoin the execution of the judgment.[4] No action lies upon it either in the state wherein it is rendered[5] or in any other state.[6] It cannot be set up as a bar in a suit upon the original cause of action.[7]

1. Pennoyer v. Neff, 95 U. S. 714, 24 L. ed. 565 (1877); Needham v. Thayer, 147 Mass. 536, 18 N. E. 429 (1888); SCOTT, CAS. CIV. PROC. 17.

2. See Elliott v. Peirsol, 1 Pet. (U. S.) 328, 340, 7 L. ed. 164 (1828).

3. McKinney v. Collins, 88 N. Y. 218 (1882).

4. Riverside, etc. Mills v. Menefee, 237 U. S. 189, 59 L. ed. 910, 35 Sup. Ct. 579 (1915).

5. Needham v. Thayer, 147 Mass. 536, 18 N. E. 429 (1888); SCOTT, CAS. CIV. PROC. 17.

6. Buchanan v. Rucker, 9 East, 191 (1808); Schibsby v. Westenholz, L. R. 6 Q. B. 155 (1870); Pennoyer v. Neff, 95 U. S. 714, 24 L. ed. 565 (1877); Rand v. Hanson, 154 Mass. 87, 28 N. E. 6 (1891); McEwan v. Zimmer, 38 Mich. 765 (1878); Whittier v. Wendell, 7 N. H. 257 (1834); Price v. Schaeffer, 161 Pa. 530, 29 Atl. 279 (1894).

7. McDonald v. Mabee, 243 U. S. 90, 61 L. ed. 608, 37 Sup. Ct. 343 (1917).

If these fundamental principles are disregarded by a state court, they may be vindicated in the federal courts, for they are protected by two provisions of the federal Constitution. If a judgment is rendered in one state and an action is brought thereon in another state, a federal question is involved under the provision of Article IV, section 1, that "full faith and credit shall be given in each state to the public acts, records and judicial proceedings of every other state."[8] The enforcement of a judgment against a defendant over whom the court has no jurisdiction involves a violation of the provision of the Fourteenth Amendment that no state shall "deprive any person of life, liberty or property without due process of law."[9] The decisions of the Supreme Court of the United States upon the question of jurisdiction over the defendant are, therefore, under these two provisions, binding upon the states.

"The foundation of jurisdiction is physical power."[10] A state cannot authorize its courts to reach out and impose liabilities upon persons over

8. Dull v. Blackman, 169 U. S. 243, 42 L. ed. 733, 18 Sup. Ct. 333 (1898); SCOTT, CAS. CIV. PROC. 670; Old Wayne Life Ass'n v. McDonough, 204 U. S. 8, 51 L. ed. 345, 27 Sup. Ct. 236 (1907).

9. Dewey v. Des Moines, 173 U. S. 193, 43 L. ed. 665, 19 Sup. Ct. 379 (1899); Simon v. Southern Ry. Co., 236 U. S. 115, 59 L. ed. 492, 35 Sup. Ct. 255 (1915); Riverside, etc. Mills v. Menefee, 237 U. S. 189, 59 L. ed. 910, 35 Sup. Ct. 579 (1915). See Pennoyer v. Neff, 95 U. S. 714, 732, 733, 24 L. ed. 565 (1877).

10. McDonald v. Mabee, 243 U. S. 90, 61 L. ed. 608, 37 Sup. Ct. 343 (1917), *per* Holmes, J.

whom the state has no control. In other jurisdictions such an attempt would be regarded as an impertinence, an unauthorized assumption of power. "Can the island of Tobago pass a law to bind the rights of the whole world?" asked Lord Ellenborough. "Would the world submit to such an assumed jurisdiction?"[11] In the leading case of *Pennoyer* v. *Neff*,[12] Mr. Justice Field said:

> "The authority of every tribunal is necessarily restricted by the territorial limits of the state in which it is established. Any attempt to exercise authority beyond those limits would be deemed in every other forum, as has been said by this court, an illegitimate assumption of power, and be resisted as mere abuse."

A state cannot compel parties domiciled in another state to leave it and respond to proceedings brought against them, or impose liabilities upon them on their failure to appear. It is immaterial whether or not the claim upon which the judgment is rendered arose within the state wherein the

11. Buchanan v. Rucker, 9 East, 191 (1808).

12. 95 U. S. 714, 720, 24 L. ed. 565 (1877). See also Baker v. Baker, Eccles & Co., 242 U. S. 394, 61 L. ed. 386, 37 Sup. Ct. 152 (1917), *per* Pitney, J.: "To hold one bound by the judgment who has not had such opportunity is contrary to the first principles of justice. And to assume that a party resident beyond the confines of a state is required to come within its borders and submit his personal controversy to its tribunals upon receiving notice of the suit at the place of his residence is a futile attempt to extend the authority and control of a state beyond its own territory."

judgment is rendered.[13] It is immaterial whether or not the defendant has property in the state,[14] although in a proceeding *in rem* or *quasi in rem,* judgment may be given against the property.[15] It is immaterial whether or not the defendant had notice of the action and an opportunity to be heard.[16] It is indeed necessary to due process that

13. Sirdar Gurgyal Singh v. Rajah of Faridkote, [1894] A. C. 670; Emanuel v. Symon, [1908] 1 K. B. 302 (C. A.). See Beale, "The Jurisdiction of Courts over Foreigners," 26 HARV. L. REV. 283, 296.

14. Pennoyer v. Neff, 95 U. S. 714, 24 L. ed. 565 (1877); Dewey v. Des Moines, 173 U. S. 193, 43 L. ed. 665, 19 Sup. Ct. 379 (1899); De Arman v. Massey, 151 Ala. 639, 44 So. 688 (1907); SCOTT, CAS. CIV. PROC. 42; Easterly v. Goodwin, 35 Conn. 273 (1868); Eastman v. Dearborn, 63 N. H. 364 (1877).

A few early cases holding that jurisdiction over the defendant's property gives jurisdiction to pronounce a personal judgment against him, have, since the decision in Pennoyer v. Neff, been discredited. De Arman v. Massey, *supra;* Laughlin v. Louisiana, etc. Co., 35 La. Ann. 1184 (1883); Lydiard v. Chute, 45 Minn. 277, 47 N. W. 967 (1891).

15. Pennoyer v. Neff, 95 U. S. 714, 24 L. ed. 565 (1877); Arndt v. Griggs, 134 U. S. 316, 33 L. ed. 918, 10 Sup. Ct. 557 (1890); Dewey v. Des Moines, 173 U. S. 193, 43 L. ed. 665, 19 Sup. Ct. 379 (1899); Clark v. Wells, 203 U. S. 164, 51 L. ed. 138, 27 Sup. Ct. 43 (1906); De Arman v. Massey, 151 Ala. 639, 44 So. 688 (1907); SCOTT, CAS. CIV. PROC. 42; Cloyd v. Trotter, 118 Ill. 391, 9 N. E. 507 (1886); SCOTT, CAS. CIV. PROC. 49; Beard v. Beard, 21 Ind. 321 (1863); Elmendorf v. Elmendorf, 58 N. J. Eq. 113, 44 Atl. 164 (1899); Schwinger v. Hickok, 53 N. Y. 280 (1873).

But such service is insufficient unless it reasonably tends to give the defendant notice and an opportunity to be heard. Roller v. Holly, 176 U. S. 398, 44 L. ed. 520, 20 Sup. Ct. 410 (1900); United States v. Fisher, 222 U. S. 204, 56 L. ed. 165, 32 Sup. Ct. 37 (1911).

16. Hence even actual service upon a nonresident defendant outside the jurisdiction is insufficient. Harkness v. Hyde, 98 U.

steps should be taken calculated to give the defendant notice and an opportunity to be heard; but something more than notice and an opportunity to be heard is necessary. The judgment is valid only when the state has some power, some control over the defendant.

The state has such control as to justify it in giving judgment in at least three cases: first, when the defendant is present within the state; second, when he has consented to the jurisdiction of the state; and third, when he is a citizen or resident of the state. If the state has control of the defendant at the time when action is brought, the jurisdiction over the defendant continues throughout all stages of the action, although the defendant may in the meantime have left the state, acquired a domicile or citizenship elsewhere, or attempted to withdraw his consent.[17]

S. 476, 25 L. ed. 237 (1878); Wilson v. Seligman, 144 U. S. 41, 36 L. ed. 338, 12 Sup. Ct. 241 (1892); Denny v. Ashley, 12 Colo. 165, 20 Pac. 331 (1888); Rand v. Hanson, 154 Mass. 87, 28 N. E. 6 (1891); McEwan v. Zimmer, 38 Mich. 765 (1878); Scott v. Streepy, 73 Texas, 547, 11 S. W. 532 (1889). Similarly, service by publication upon a nonresident is insufficient. Freeman v. Alderson, 119 U. S. 185, 30 L. ed. 372, 7 Sup. Ct. 165 (1886); Baker v. Baker, Eccles & Co., 242 U. S. 394, 61 L. ed. 386, 37 Sup. Ct. 152 (1917); Cocke v. Brewer, 68 Miss. 775, 9 So. 823 (1891); Smith v. McCutchen, 38 Mo. 415 (1866); McKinney v. Collins, 88 N. Y. 216 (1882); Hanna v. Stedman, 230 N. Y. 326, 130 N. E. 566 (1921). Compare D'Arcy v. Ketchum, 11 How. (U. S.) 165, 13 L. ed. 648 (1850) (service upon a co-debtor).

17. Nations v. Johnson, 24 How. (U. S.) 195, 16 L. ed. 628 (1860); Michigan Trust Co. v. Ferry, 228 U. S. 346, 57 L. ed. 867, 33 Sup. Ct. 550 (1913); Fitzsimmons v. Johnson, 90 Tenn.

The most usual method of acquiring jurisdiction is by personal service of process upon the defendant. Such service is valid only when the defendant, whether a resident or nonresident, is within the state when served. While he is within the state, no matter for how brief a time, the state has control over him, and if during that time he is duly served with process, the court acquires jurisdiction over him,[18] unless indeed for some reason he was exempt or privileged from service.[19]

Again, jurisdiction over the person of the defendant may be acquired by his consent. This consent may be given either before or after action has been brought. Jurisdiction is conferred when the defendant enters a general appearance in an action, that is, an appearance for some purpose other than that of raising the objection of lack of

416, 17 S. W. 100 (1891). ''This is one of the decencies of civilization that no one would dispute.'' Michigan Trust Co. v. Ferry, *supra, per* Holmes, J. As to the extent of this principle, see New York Life Ins. Co. v. Dunlevy, 241 U. S. 518, 60 L. ed. 1140, 36 Sup. Ct. 613 (1916).

18. Smith v. Gibson, 83 Ala. 284, 3 So. 321 (1887); SCOTT, CAS. CIV. PROC. 20; Lee v. Baird, 139 Ala. 526, 36 So. 720 (1903); Darrah v. Watson, 36 Iowa, 116 (1872); Alley v. Caspari, 80 Me. 234, 14 Atl. 12 (1888); Peabody v. Hamilton, 106 Mass. 217 (1870); Thompson v. Cowell, 148 Mass. 552, 20 N. E. 170 (1889).

19. As in the case of persons inveigled into the state, and nonresident witnesses and, in some jurisdictions, nonresident parties to judicial proceedings. Stewart v. Ramsay, 242 U. S. 128, 61 L. ed. 192, 37 Sup. Ct. 44 (1916); Matthews v. Tufts, 87 N. Y. 568 (1882). As to privilege from service of process, see also cases cited in SCOTT, CAS. CIV. PROC. 23.

jurisdiction over him.[20]   A stipulation waiving service has the same effect.[21]   The defendant may, before suit is brought, give a power of attorney to confess judgment,[22] or appoint an agent to accept service, or agree that service by any other method

20. Boyle v. Sacker, 39 Ch. D. 249 (C. A. 1888); Henderson v. Carbondale, etc. Co., 142 U. S. 25, 35 L. ed. 332, 11 Sup. Ct. 691 (1891); Western Loan Co. v. Butte, etc. Co., 210 U. S. 368, 52 L. ed. 1101, 28 Sup. Ct. 720 (1908); St. Louis Car Co. v. Stillwater, etc. Co., 53 Minn. 129, 54 N. W. 1064 (1893); Scott, Cas. Civ. Proc. 57. An application for an extension of time to answer is not necessarily a general appearance. Meisukas v. Greenough, etc. Co., 244 U. S. 54, 61 L. ed. 987, 37 Sup. Ct. 593 (1917); Lowrie v. Castle, 198 Mass. 82, 83 N. E. 1118 (1908). A petition for removal to a federal court is not a general appearance. Goldey v. Morning News, 156 U. S. 518, 39 L. ed. 517, 15 Sup. Ct. 559 (1895); Wabash Western Ry. v. Brow, 164 U. S. 271, 41 L. ed. 431, 17 Sup. Ct. 126 (1896); Mechanical Appliance Co. v. Castleman, 215 U. S. 437, 54 L. ed. 272, 30 Sup. Ct. 125 (1910). A state statute providing that an appearance for any purpose confers jurisdiction over the defendant is constitutional. York v. Texas, 137 U. S. 15, 34 L. ed. 580, 11 Sup. Ct. 6 (1890); Scott, Cas. Civ. Proc. 64. *Cf.* Harris v. Taylor, [1915] 2 K. B. 580.

21. Allured v. Voller, 107 Mich. 476, 65 N. W. 285 (1895); Scott, Cas. Civ. Proc. 30; Jones v. Merrill, 113 Mich. 433, 71 N. W. 838 (1897).

22. Van Norman v. Gordon, 172 Mass. 576, 53 N. E. 267 (1899); First National Bank v. Garland, 109 Mich. 515, 67 N. W. 559 (1896); Hazel v. Jacobs, 78 N. J. L. 459, 75 Atl. 903 (1910); Scott, Cas. Civ. Proc. 550; Teel v. Yost, 128 N. Y. 387, 28 N. E. 353 (1891). The judgment is not valid unless the authority given in the power of attorney is strictly followed. Grover, etc. Co. v. Radcliffe, 137 U. S. 287, 34 L. ed. 670, 11 Sup. Ct. 92 (1890); National Exchange Bank v. Wiley, 195 U. S. 257, 49 L. ed. 184, 25 Sup. Ct. 70 (1904); *Re* Raymor's Estate, 165 Mich. 259, 130 N. W. 594 (1911).

shall be sufficient.[23] The defendant in all these cases has submitted to the control of the state and of the court over him.

Again, a state has control over its citizens and over all persons domiciled within the state even when they have gone outside the state. At common law jurisdiction over such persons can be acquired by the courts of the state only by personal service within the state, or by consent.[24] But statutes in several states have provided for other methods of service upon citizens and residents. If the methods provided for are such as are reasonably calculated to give notice and an opportunity to defend, they are constitutional.[25]

23. Montgomery, Jones & Co. v. Liebenthal & Co., [1898] 1 Q. B. 487 (C. A.); SCOTT, CAS. CIV. PROC. 27.

24. At common law if no service could be made upon a resident it was possible to outlaw him. 3 BL. COMM. *283. One result of the outlawry was to forfeit to the Crown the property of the defendant. This did not directly inure to the benefit of the plaintiff, but it was a powerful club to force the defendant to appear. The process of outlawry was rejected in the United States as inapplicable to our conditions. Blessing v. McLinden, 81 N. J. L. 379, 79 Atl. 347 (1911); SCOTT, CAS. CIV. PROC. 146; Nathanson v. Spitz, 19 R. I. 70, 31 Atl. 690 (1895); McCall v. Price, 1 McCord (S. C.) 82 (1821); SCOTT, CAS. CIV. PROC. 143.

In European countries jurisdiction is normally based upon allegiance or domicile rather than upon the personal presence of the defendant. Beale, ''The Jurisdiction of Courts over Foreigners,'' 26 HARV. L. REV. 193.

25. Ouseley v. Lehigh Valley, etc. Co., 84 Fed. 602 (C. C., E. D. Pa., 1897); Bickerdike v. Allen, 157 Ill. 95, 41 N. E. 740 (1895) (publication and mailing); Sturgis v. Fay, 16 Ind. 429 (1861) (usual or last place of residence); Bryant v. Shute's Executor, 147 Ky. 268, 144 S. W. 28 (1912) (last and usual place of abode); Harryman v. Roberts, 52 Md. 64 (1879) (service at

To what extent has a state control over non-residents not personally within the state but doing business therein, either as individuals or as partners? To what extent may the state confer upon its courts jurisdiction over such persons? In *Pennoyer* v. *Neff*,[26] in which the general principles in regard to jurisdiction were thoroughly discussed and expounded, these questions were expressly left open. Mr. Justice Field said:[27]

> "Neither do we mean to assert that a state may not require a nonresident entering into a partnership or association within its limits, or making contracts enforceable there, to appoint an agent or representative in the state to receive service of process and notice in

residence); Henderson v. Staniford, 105 Mass. 504 (1870) (publication); Continental National Bank v. Thurber, 74 Hun (N. Y.) 632, 26 N. Y. Supp. 956 (1893) (service at residence); SCOTT, CAS. CIV. PROC. 31. *Cf.* Douglas v. Forrest, 4 Bing. 686 (1828) (proclamation in public place); Schibsby v. Westenholz, L. R. 6 Q. B. 155 (1870). But see, *contra,* Raher v. Raher, 150 Iowa, 511, 129 N. W. 494 (1911) (service outside the state).

A method of service is insufficient when, although it may have a tendency to give notice to the defendant, yet there is another way obviously better calculated to give notice. Service by publication is insufficient therefore when personal service is possible (Bardwell v. Collins, 44 Minn. 97, 46 N. W. 315 [1890]), or when the defendant had left the state but his family remained at his last place of abode. McDonald v. Mabee, 243 U. S. 90, 61 L. ed. 608, 37 Sup. Ct. 343 (1917). It is doubtful whether service by publication upon a resident is sufficient even when no other method of service is available. See McDonald v. Mabee, *supra;* De la Montanya v. De la Montanya, 112 Cal. 104, 44 Pac. 354 (1896).

26. 95 U. S. 714, 24 L. ed. 565 (1877).

27. 95 U. S. 735.

legal proceedings instituted with respect to such partnership, association, or contracts, or to designate a place where such service may be made and notice given, and provide, upon their failure to make such appointment or to designate such place, that service may be made upon a public officer designated for that purpose, or in some other prescribed way, and that judgments rendered upon such service may not be binding upon the nonresidents both within and without the state.''

A number of cases have lately arisen involving the validity of a Kentucky statute. This statute [28] provides that:

"In actions against an individual residing in another state, or a partnership, association, or joint stock company, the members of which reside in another state, engaged in business in this state, the summons may be served on the manager, or agent of, or person in charge of, such business in this state, in the county where the business is carried on, or in the county where the cause of action occurred."

The courts of Kentucky have upheld the validity of this statute.[29] In several cases, however, the

---

28. KENTUCKY CIVIL CODE, § 51, subsec. 6.

29. Guenther v. American Steel Hoop Co., 116 Ky. 580, 76 S. W. 419 (1903); Johnson v. Westerfield, 143 Ky. 10, 135 S. W. 425 (1911); Crane v. Hall, 165 Ky. 827, 178 S. W. 1096 (1915).

courts of other states have held invalid Kentucky judgments rendered under the statute.[30]

In the most recent of these cases, *Flexner* v. *Farson*,[31] an action of debt was brought in Illinois upon a Kentucky judgment. It appeared that the cause of action on which the judgment was based arose in Kentucky; that the defendants were non-residents, but were, at the time the cause of action arose, doing business in Kentucky as partners through one Washington Flexner as their agent; that service was made upon him after he had ceased to act as such agent; that the defendants did not appear in the action; and that the Kentucky court thereupon rendered judgment against them by default. The Illinois court gave judgment for the defendants, which was affirmed on appeal by the Supreme Court of the state. The plaintiff, contending that full faith and credit was

30. Moredock v. Kirby, 118 Fed. 180 (C. C., W. D. Ky., 1902); Flexner v. Farson, 268 Ill. 435, 109 N. E. 327 (1915); Cabanne v. Graf, 87 Minn. 510, 92 N. W. 461 (1902); Scott, Cas. Civ. Proc. 24; Carroll v. Curran, 193 N. Y. App. D. 948, 184 N. Y. Supp. 603 (1920). For cases holding similar statutes invalid, see Brooks v. Dun, 51 Fed. 138 (C. C., W. D. Tenn., 1892); Ralya Market Co. v. Armour & Co., 102 Fed. 530 (C. C., N. D. Iowa, 1900); Caldwell v. Armour, 1 Pen. (Del.) 545 (1899); Aikmann v. Sanderson, 122 La. 265, 47 So. 600 (1908); Knox Bros. v. Wagner & Co., 141 Tenn. 348, 209 S. W. 638 (1919). But see, *contra*, Alaska Commercial Co. v. Debney, 144 Fed. 1, 75 C. C. A. 131 (1906); Rauber v. Whitney, 125 Ind. 216, 25 N. E. 186 (1890); Behn v. Whitney, 125 Ind. 599, 25 N. E. 187 (1890); Edwards v. Van Cleave, 47 Ind. App. 347, 94 N. E. 596 (1911); Victor Cornille & De Blonde v. Dun & Co., 143 La. 1045, 79 So. 855 (1918); Green v. Snyder, 114 Tenn. 100, 84 S. W. 808 (1904).

31. 268 Ill. 435, 109 N. E. 327 (1915).

denied to the Kentucky judgment, brought the case on writ of error to the Supreme Court of the United States, and that court has affirmed the Illinois judgment.[32] The opinion of the court, delivered by Mr. Justice Holmes, is very brief. After stating the facts, he says:

"It is argued that the pleas tacitly admit that Washington Flexner was agent of the firm at the time of the transaction sued upon in Kentucky, and the Kentucky statute is construed as purporting to make him agent to receive service in suits arising out of the business done in that state. On this construction it is said that the defendants by doing business in the state consented to be bound by the service prescribed. The analogy of suits against insurance companies based upon such service is invoked. *Mutual Reserve Fund Life Association* v. *Phelps,* 190 U. S. 147. But the consent that is said to be implied in such cases is a mere fiction, founded upon the accepted doctrine that the states could exclude foreign corporations altogether, and therefore could establish this obligation as a condition to letting them in. *Lafayette Ins. Co.* v. *French,* 18 How. 404; *Pennsylvania Fire Ins. Co.* v. *Gold Issue Mining & Milling Co.,* 243 U. S. 93, 96. The state had no power to

32. Flexner v. Farson, 248 U. S. 289, 63 L. ed. 250, 39 Sup. Ct. 97 (1919). The decision is approved by Professor Beale. 33 HARV. L. REV. 1, 9. See 34 HARV. L. REV. 55-56.

exclude the defendants and on that ground without going farther the Supreme Court of Illinois rightly held that the analogy failed, and that the Kentucky judgment was void. If the Kentucky statute purports to have the effect attributed to it, it cannot have that effect in the present case. *New York Life Ins. Co.* v. *Dunlevy,* 241 U. S. 518, 522, 523. Judgment affirmed.''

The line of thought which the opinion seems to suggest is this: A state may exclude a foreign corporation altogether, and may therefore admit it on such conditions as it may choose to impose; but a state may not exclude nonresident individuals, and may not therefore impose any conditions on admission. The problem, however, is not quite as simple as this. A state may not always exclude foreign corporations; for example, it may not exclude a corporation which seeks to do only an interstate business. But even though it may not exclude, it may impose some conditions on admission.[33]

33. See International Harvester Co. v. Kentucky, 234 U. S. 579, 58 L. ed. 1479, 34 Sup. Ct. 944 (1914), stated and discussed *infra,* p. 58.

And even though a state may exclude, there are some conditions on admission it may not impose, *e. g.* conditions designed to prevent resorting to the federal courts or conditions which would result in taking the property of the corporation without due process of law. See note 44, *infra.* But see the dissenting opinion of Mr. Justice Holmes in Western Union Tel. Co. v. Kansas, 216 U. S. 1, 52, 54 L. ed. 355, 30 Sup. Ct. 190 (1910). For a discussion of ''unconstitutional conditions,'' see HENDERSON,

The opinion of Mr. Justice Holmes suggests an inquiry into the basis of jurisdiction over corporations. There is no difficulty as to domestic corporations. Obviously the state which creates a corporation has the necessary control over it to serve as a basis of jurisdiction. It is domiciled within the state. At common law service upon a corporation is effected by service upon its principal officer.[34] By statute service upon other officers or agents is frequently allowed, and such service, or service by any other method, is valid if it fairly tends to give the corporation notice of the action and an opportunity to be heard.[35]

A more difficult question arises as to foreign corporations, that is, corporations organized and

POSITION OF FOREIGN CORPORATIONS IN AMERICAN CONSTITUTIONAL LAW, chap. VIII; Report of the Commissioner of Corporations on State Laws concerning Foreign Corporations, 1915, Pt. II.

34. Kansas City, etc. R. R. Co. v. Daughtry, 138 U. S. 298, 305, 34 L. ed. 963, 11 Sup. Ct. 306 (1891); State v. Western N. C. R. R. Co., 89 N. C. 584 (1883); 1 TIDD, PRACTICE, 9 ed., 121.

35. St. Mary's Petroleum Co. v. West Virginia, 203 U. S. 183, 51 L. ed. 144, 27 Sup. Ct. 132 (1906) (service upon state auditor); Clearwater Mercantile Co. v. Roberts, 51 Fla. 176, 40 So. 436 (1906) (publication); SCOTT, CAS. CIV. PROC. 34; Nelson v. C., B. & Q. R. R. Co., 225 Ill. 197, 80 N. E. 109 (1907) (publication and mail); Hinckley v. Kettle River R. R. Co., 70 Minn. 105, 72 N. W. 835 (1897) (deposit of summons in office of secretary of state, who is charged with duty of mailing a copy to an officer of the corporation); Straub v. Lyman, etc. Co., 30 S. D. 310, 138 N. W. 957 (1912) (service outside the state).

If the method of service is not reasonably calculated to give the corporation notice and an opportunity to defend, it is unconstitutional. Pinney v. Providence Loan & Investment Co., 106 Wis. 396, 82 N. W. 308 (1900) (leaving copy in registry of deeds, no one being charged with duty to notify defendant).

existing under the laws of another state or territory or country than that in which the action is brought. If a foreign corporation is not doing business within the state, it is not subject to the jurisdiction of the state merely because one or more of its officers or agents happens to live there or to go there.[36] The New York and North Carolina courts long obstinately clung to the opposite view;[37] but the Supreme Court of the United States has now definitely held that a state has no jurisdiction over the corporation in such a case, and that an attempt to exercise jurisdiction is a violation of the Fourteenth Amendment.[38]

Certainly, however, a foreign corporation may voluntarily consent to submit itself to the jurisdiction of the state and of the courts of the state. And inasmuch as a corporation, although a "person"[39] and entitled as such to protection under

36. St. Clair v. Cox, 106 U. S. 350, 27 L. ed. 222, 1 Sup. Ct. 354 (1882); Goldey v. Morning News, 156 U. S. 518, 39 L. ed. 517, 15 Sup. Ct. 559 (1895); Kendall v. American Automatic Loom Co., 198 U. S. 477, 49 L. ed. 1133, 25 Sup. Ct. 768 (1905); SCOTT, CAS. CIV. PROC. 39; Newell v. Great W. Ry. Co., 19 Mich 336 (1869); Moulin v. Insurance Co., 24 N. J. L. (4 Zab.) 222 (1853); Aldrich v. Anchor Coal Co., 24 Ore. 32, 32 Pac. 756 (1893).

37. Sadler v. Boston, etc. Co., 202 N. Y. 547, 95 N. E. 1139 (1911), 140 N. Y. App. Div. 367, 125 N. Y. Supp. 405 (1910); SCOTT, CAS. CIV. PROC. 40; Menefee v. Riverside, etc. Mills, 161 N. C. 164, 76 S. E. 741 (1913).

38. Riverside, etc. Mills v. Menefee, 237 U. S. 189, 59 L. ed. 910, 35 Sup. Ct. 579 (1915). See also Dollar Co. v. Canadian, etc. Co., 220 N. Y. 270, 115 N. E. 711 (1917).

39. Santa Clara Co. v. Southern Pac. R. R. Co., 118 U. S. 394,

the due-process clause of the Fourteenth Amendment, is not a "citizen"[40] and is not as such entitled to "all privileges and immunities of citizens
in the several states,"[41] or "the privileges or immunities of citizens of the United States,"[42] a
state may in general exclude a foreign corporation from doing business within the state.[43] It
may impose conditions precedent to its doing
business within the state. It may impose as a
condition precedent the filing of a consent to service of process in a designated manner. If a foreign corporation actually files such a consent it
is bound thereby.[44]

396, 30 L. ed. 118, 6 Sup. Ct. 1132 (1886); Smyth v. Ames, 169 U.
S. 466, 42 L. ed. 819, 18 Sup. Ct. 418 (1898).

40. Paul v. Virginia, 8 Wall. (U. S.) 168, 19 L. ed. 357 (1868).

41. Article IV, § 2.

42. Amendment XIV.

43. Paul v. Virginia, 8 Wall. (U. S.) 168, 19 L. ed. 357 (1868).
For an exhaustive digest of decisions as to what constitutes
"doing business" within a state, see the Report of the Commissioner of Corporations on State Laws concerning Foreign
Corporations, 1915, 156-68.

44. The decisions on this point are numberless. See BEALE,
FOREIGN CORPORATIONS, chaps. VII, XI; HENDERSON, POSITION
OF FOREIGN CORPORATIONS IN AMERICAN CONSTITUTIONAL LAW,
chap. V.

But a foreign corporation is not bound by its consent to conditions which are so outrageously unreasonable as to amount to
a deprivation of property without due process of law. "A state
may not say to a foreign corporation, you may do business within
our borders if you permit your property to be taken without due
process of law." Baltic Mining Co. v. Massachusetts, 231 U. S.
68, 83, 58 L. ed. 127, 34 Sup. Ct. 15 (1913). It is conceived
therefore that if the corporation should agree to be bound by a
judgment rendered without any service of process, or after ser-

Not infrequently it happens that a foreign corporation does business in a state without having filed consent to any form of service of process. The statute may not require the filing of any consent, but may simply provide that if a corporation does business within the state, service may be made upon one of its officers or agents within the state, or upon a public officer of the state. Or the statute may require the filing of a consent, but the corporation may have neglected to comply with the statute.[45] In such cases, where the corporation has not expressly assented to the jurisdiction of the state and of the courts of the state, three possible foundations for jurisdiction have been suggested: (1) that the corporation has given an "implied" consent to the jurisdiction; (2) that the corporation is present and is found within the state; and (3) that on principles of justice, if a corporation voluntarily does business within the state, it is bound by the reasonable regulations by the state of that business.[46]

1. In the leading case of *Lafayette Insurance Co.* v. *French,*[47] jurisdiction is rested upon the

vice by a method which would have no tendency to give notice of the action to the corporation or an opportunity to be heard, it would not be bound. See note 33, *supra,* and note 50, *infra.*

45. For a summary of the statutes of the several states, see the Report of the Commissioner of Corporations on State Laws concerning Foreign Corporations, 1915, 34-41.

46. A corporation, it seems clear, is domiciled only in the state creating it. Hence jurisdiction over a foreign corporation cannot be based upon domicile.

47. 18 How. (U. S.) 404, 15 L. ed. 451 (1855).

theory of "implied" consent. Mr. Justice Curtis said:[48]

> "A corporation created by Indiana can transact business in Ohio only with the consent, express or implied, of the latter state. 13 Pet. 519. This consent may be accompanied by such conditions as Ohio may think fit to impose; and these conditions must be deemed valid and effectual by other states, and by this court, provided they are not repugnant to the constitution or laws of the United States, or inconsistent with those rules of public law which secure the jurisdiction and authority of each state from encroachment by all others, or that principle of natural justice which forbids condemnation without opportunity for defence. . . . Now, when this corporation sent its agent into Ohio, with authority to make contracts of insurance there, the corporation must be taken to assent to the condition upon which alone such business could be there transacted by them; that condition being, that an agent, to make contracts, should also be the agent of the corporation to receive service of process in suits on such contracts."

This line of reasoning is undoubtedly sound enough in cases in which it is really possible to find sufficient evidence of consent. In truth, how-

48. 18 How. 407, 408.

ever, although it is sometimes possible to spell out a consent by the corporation, it is often difficult and sometimes impossible to do so.[49] But the corporation may be held even if it appears that it did not consent. The Supreme Court recognizes that the implication of consent in many cases involves a fiction, but the corporation nevertheless does not on that account escape.[50]

2. To meet the difficulty of lack of any real consent, and to avoid the necessity of resorting to a fiction, it has been urged that the jurisdiction is based upon the presence of the corporation within the state.[51] It is asserted that a corporation is actually present and can be found wherever it is

49. The difficulties with the theory of implied consent are set forth in HENDERSON, POSITION OF FOREIGN CORPORATIONS IN AMERICAN CONSTITUTIONAL LAW, chap. V; Cahill, ''Jurisdiction over Foreign Corporations,'' 30 HARV. L. REV. 676. The theory is supported in BEALE, FOREIGN CORPORATIONS, chap. XI.

50. Conversely, a foreign corporation is not bound by regulations which are so outrageous as to amount to a deprivation of property without due process of law. It has been held that if a state statute provides for service of process upon a foreign corporation doing business within the state by service upon a public officer, such service is invalid if it is not such as is calculated to give notice to the corporation. King Tonopah Mining Co. v. Lynch, 232 Fed. 485 (D. C., Nev., 1916) (service upon state official not charged with duty to notify corporation); Knapp v. Bullock Tractor Co., 242 Fed. 543 (D. C., S. D. Cal., 1917) (like preceding case). Cf. Mutual Life Ins. Co. v. Spratley, 172 U. S. 602, 43 L. ed. 569, 19 Sup. Ct. 308 (1899); Commercial Mutual Accident Co. v. Davis, 213 U. S. 245, 53 L. ed. 782, 29 Sup. Ct. 445 (1909).

51. For a discussion of this theory, see HENDERSON, POSITION OF FOREIGN CORPORATIONS IN AMERICAN CONSTITUTIONAL LAW, chap. V; 30 HARV. L. REV. 676-96.

engaged in business. On this theory a foreign corporation can be served in a state where it does business even though no statute authorizes such service. Some cases have indeed gone to this length.[52] There would seem to be no objection on principle to this theory, but it has never met with complete and unqualified approval by the Supreme Court. In a famous dictum of Chief Justice Taney in *Bank of Augusta* v. *Earle*,[53] the proposition was asserted in broad terms that "a corporation can have no legal existence out of the boundaries of the sovereignty by which it is created." Although since that dictum was promulgated, the broad doctrine there laid down has been considerably limited, and the Supreme Court has in many cases stated that a corporation may be found outside the state wherein it was organized, yet the Supreme Court has never completely and definitely repudiated the dictum. Two recent cases, *Old Wayne Life Association* v. *McDonough*[54] and *Simon* v. *Southern Railway*,[55] decided by that court, tend to show a disapproval of, or at least a limitation on, the doctrine of corporate presence. In these cases it was held that under a statute providing for service on foreign corporations

---

52. La Compagnie Générale Transatlantique v. Law & Co., [1899] A. C. 431; Wilson Packing Co. v. Hunter, 8 Biss. 429, Fed. Cas. No. 17,852 (1879). But see Desper v. Continental Water Meter Co., 137 Mass. 252 (1884). And see cases cited, SCOTT, CAS. CIV. PROC. 38, note.

53. 13 Pet. (U. S.) 519, 588, 10 L. ed. 274 (1839).

54. 204 U. S. 8, 51 L. ed. 345, 27 Sup. Ct. 236 (1907).

55. 236 U. S. 115, 59 L. ed. 492, 35 Sup. Ct. 255 (1915).

doing business within the state by service upon a public official, such service was insufficient if the cause of action arose in another state.

3. In explanation of *Old Wayne Life Association* v. *McDonough* and *Simon* v. *Southern Railway*, Learned Hand, J., has, in the case of *Smolik* v. *Philadelphia & Reading Coal & Iron Co.*,[56] suggested a third possible theory on which to base jurisdiction over foreign corporations. In that case it appeared that a New York statute required every foreign corporation doing business in New York to take out a license, which should not be issued unless the corporation had appointed an agent within the state upon whom process might be served. The defendant corporation did appoint such an agent, and in an action brought in the federal District Court for the Southern District of New York, and based upon a cause of action which did not arise in New York, service was made upon the agent. A motion to set aside the service was denied.[57] Judge Hand said:

> "When it is said that a foreign corporation will be taken to have consented to the appointment of an agent to accept service, the court does not mean that as a fact it has consented at all, because the corporation does not in fact consent; but the court, for purposes of justice, treats it as if it had. It is true that the con-

56. 222 Fed. 148 (D. C., S. D., N. Y., 1915).

57. Bagdon v. Philadelphia, etc. Co., 217 N. Y. 432, 111 N. E. 1075 (1916), *accord*.

sequences so imputed to it lie within its own control, since it need not do business within the state, but that is not equivalent to a consent; actually it might have refused to appoint, and yet its refusal would make no difference. The court, in the interests of justice, imputes results to the voluntary act of doing business within the foreign state, quite independently of any intent.

"The limits of that consent are as independent of any actual intent as the consent itself. Being a mere creature of justice it will have such consent only as justice requires; hence it may be limited, as it has been limited in *Simon* v. *Southern Railway, supra,* and *Old Wayne Insurance Co.* v. *McDonough, supra.* The actual consent in the cases at bar has no such latitudinarian possibilities; it must be measured by the proper meaning to be attributed to the words used, and, where that meaning calls for wide application, such must be given."[58]

---

58. 222 Fed. 148, 151. This opinion was approved by Holmes, J., in Pennsylvania Fire Ins. Co. v. Gold Issue Min. & Mill. Co., 243 U. S. 93, 61 L. ed. 610, 37 Sup. Ct. 344 (1917), in which case the defendant had filed a consent to service of process upon a *public official,* and the service was upheld although the cause of action arose outside the state. It is not yet settled whether, in view of the Old Wayne and Simon cases, service of process upon an *agent* is valid, when the cause of action arose outside the state, if no consent had been filed. The service was held invalid in Fry v. Denver, etc. R. R. Co., 226 Fed. 893 (D. C., N. D., Cal., 1915), and in Takacs v. Philadelphia, etc. Ry. Co., 228 Fed. 728 (D. C., S. D., N. Y., 1915). But the contrary result was reached

Here then is a third theory of the basis of jurisdiction over foreign corporations. If a foreign
corporation voluntarily does business within the
state it is bound by reasonable regulations of that
business imposed by the state, not because it is
found there, not because it has consented to those
regulations, but because it is as reasonable and
just to subject the corporation to those regulations as though it had consented. The jurisdiction is based upon the control of the state resulting from the voluntary act of the corporation in
doing business within the state, not from its voluntary consent to be bound by the laws of the
state.[59]   Here is no illegitimate assumption of
power by the state; Tobago is not trying to bind
the rights of the whole world.

in Barrow Steamship Co. v. Kane, 170 U. S. 100, 42 L. ed. 964, **18**
Sup. Ct. 526 (1898); Atchison, etc. Ry. Co. v. Weeks, 248 **Fed.**
970, 979 (D. C., W. D., Texas, 1918); Reynolds v. Missouri, **etc.**
Ry., 228 Mass. 584, 117 N. E. 913 (1917); Tauza v. Susquehanna
Coal Co., 220 N. Y. 259, 115 N. E. 915 (1917).

59. A state may validly provide for service of process upon **a**
foreign corporation which has ceased to do business within **the**
state if the cause of action arose in the state before the with-
drawal.   Mutual Reserve Life, etc. Ass'n v. Phelps, 190 U. **S.**
147, 47 L. ed. 987, 23 Sup. Ct. 707 (1903); McCord Lumber Co.
v. Doyle, 97 Fed. 22, 38 C. C. A. 34 (1899); Tucker v. Insurance Co., 232 Mass. 224, 122 N. E. 285 (1919).   *Cf.* Hunter v.
Mutual Reserve Life Ins. Co., 218 U. S. 573, 54 L. ed. 1155, 31
Sup. Ct. 127 (1910).   It would be impossible to say that **at**
the time of service the corporation is present within the state.
People's Tobacco Co. v. American Tobacco Co., 246 U. S. **79,**
62 L. ed. 587, 38 Sup. Ct. 233 (1918).   These decisions **can be**
upheld only on the theory of implied consent, or on the **theory**
suggested by Judge Hand.

Having examined the possible bases of jurisdiction over foreign corporations, we may turn again to the question of jurisdiction over nonresident persons.[60] When citizens of other states seek to do business within the state, either as individuals or as partners, the state has no power arbitrarily to exclude them. To do so would violate the provision of Article IV, section 2, of the federal Constitution that "The citizens of each state shall be entitled to all privileges and immunities of citizens in the several states"; and the provision of the Fourteenth Amendment that "No state shall make or enforce any law which shall abridge the privileges or immunities of citizens of the United States." But because the state cannot exclude, it does not follow that it may not impose conditions upon admission.

It is well settled that a state may, in the reasonable exercise of the police power, regulate business carried on within the state, although the business is of an interstate character and although it is carried on by nonresidents. Under the pretence of exercising the police power, to be sure, the state

60. I have not attempted to distinguish cases where the business is carried on by a partnership from those in which it is carried on by an individual. In our law a partnership is not treated as an entity. If it were so treated it would be possible to apply many of the principles applicable to corporations which are not applicable to individuals. See Worcester, etc. Co. v. Firbank, Pauling & Co., [1894] 1 Q. B. 784; Von Hellfeld v. Richnitzer and Mayers Frères & Co., [1914] 1 Ch. 748; Sugg v. Thornton, 132 U. S. 524, 33 L. ed. 447, 10 Sup. Ct. 163 (1889); State v. Adams Express Co., 66 Minn. 271, 68 N. W. 1085 (1896).

may not impose burdens upon interstate commerce, or take property without due process of law, or deny to any person within its jurisdiction the equal protection of the laws, or deny to citizens of the several states and citizens of the United States the privileges and immunities guaranteed by the Constitution. When a state attempts to compel nonresidents doing business within the state to submit to the jurisdiction of the courts of the state, the validity of the attempt depends upon the question whether this is a reasonable exercise of the power to regulate business.

The state has not power to exclude a corporation which seeks to do within the state only interstate business. Nevertheless it was held in *International Harvester Co.* v. *Kentucky*[61] that the state may validly provide that such a corporation should appoint an agent to accept service of process. Such a provision does not impose an improper burden upon interstate commerce. It merely treats foreign corporations like domestic corporations. Mr. Justice Day, speaking for the court in that case, said:

"It is argued that a corporation engaged in purely interstate commerce within a state cannot be required to submit to regulations such as designating an agent upon whom process may be served as a condition of doing such business, and that as such requirement cannot be made, the ordinary agents of the

61. 234 U. S. 579, 58 L. ed. 1479, 34 Sup. Ct. 944 (1914).

corporation, although doing interstate business within the state, cannot by its laws be made amenable to judicial process within the state. The contention comes to this, so long as a foreign corporation engages in interstate commerce only it is immune from the service of process under the laws of the state in which it is carrying on such business. This is indeed, as was said by the Court of Appeals of Kentucky, a novel proposition, and we are unable to find a decision to support it, nor has one been called to our attention. True, it has been held time and again that a state cannot burden interstate commerce or pass laws which amount to the regulation of such commerce; but this is a long way from holding that the ordinary process of the courts may not reach corporations carrying on business within the state which is wholly of an interstate commerce character.''[62]

62. A statute subjecting cars used in interstate commerce to attachment and garnishment is not an improper interference with interstate commerce. Davis v. Cleveland, etc. Ry. Co., 217 U. S. 157, 54 L. ed. 708, 30 Sup. Ct. 463 (1910).

A state may not impose unreasonable conditions upon a corporation seeking to carry on within the state only interstate commerce. International Textbook Co. v. Pigg, 217 U. S. 91, 54 L. ed. 678, 30 Sup. Ct. 481 (1910); Sioux Remedy Co. v. Cope, 235 U. S. 197, 59 L. ed. 193, 35 Sup. Ct. 57 (1914). But it may impose such conditions upon a corporation seeking to carry on intrastate as well as interstate commerce, provided the conditions do not actually burden interstate commerce. Interstate Amusement Co. v. Albert, 239 U. S. 560, 60 L. ed. 439, 36 Sup. Ct. 168 (1916). It may not, however, impose conditions upon a

Although the state may not exclude the corporation, it may compel the corporation to submit to the jurisdiction of its courts.

The case of *Kane* v. *New Jersey* [63] shows that although a state may not exclude from its borders a nonresident individual, yet it may under certain circumstances impose as a condition of admission the appointment of an agent to accept service of process. A statute of New Jersey provided that a nonresident owner of an automobile should, as a condition precedent to his right to operate his car in the highways of the state, appoint the secretary of state as his agent upon whom process might be served "in any action or legal proceeding caused by the operation of his registered motor vehicle within this state against such owner." The defendant, a resident of New York, having failed to comply with this provision was arrested while driving his automobile in New Jersey. When arrested he was on his way from New York to Pennsylvania. He claimed that the statute as to him violated the Constitution and

corporation seeking to carry on intrastate as well as interstate commerce if the conditions would operate as a burden upon interstate commerce. Western Union Tel. Co. v. Kansas, 216 U. S. 1, 54 L. ed. 355, 30 Sup. Ct. 190 (1910); Pullman Co. v. Kansas, 216 U. S. 56, 54 L. ed. 378, 30 Sup. Ct. 232 (1910); Ludwig v. Western Union Tel. Co., 216 U. S. 146, 54 L. ed. 423, 30 Sup. Ct. 280 (1910); Looney v. Crane Co., 245 U. S. 178, 62 L. ed. 230, 38 Sup. Ct. 85 (1917); International Paper Co. v. Massachusetts, 246 U. S. 135, 62 L. ed. 624, 38 Sup. Ct. 292. *Cf.* Interstate Amusement Co. v. Albert, 239 U. S. 560, 60 L. ed. 439, 36 Sup. Ct. 168 (1916).

63. 242 U. S. 160, 61 L. ed. 222, 37 Sup. Ct. 30 (1916).

laws of the United States regulating interstate
commerce, and also the Fourteenth Amendment.
These contentions were overruled, and he was
fined. The conviction was affirmed in the highest
court of the state, and the case was brought to the
Supreme Court of the United States by writ of
error. It was held that the statute was constitutional. Mr. Justice Brandeis, speaking for the
court, said:[64]

"We know that ability to enforce criminal
and civil penalties for transgression is an aid
to securing observance of laws. And in view
of the speed of the automobile and the habits
of men, we cannot say that the Legislature
of New Jersey was unreasonable in believing
that ability to establish, by legal proceedings
within the state, any financial liability of nonresident owners, was essential to public
safety. There is nothing to show that the
requirement is unduly burdensome in practice. It is not a discrimination against nonresidents, denying them equal protection of
the law. On the contrary, it puts nonresident
owners upon an equality with resident
owners."

A state may then in the exercise of its police
power impose reasonable conditions upon nonresidents wishing to do acts within the state. The
mere fact that the state may not prevent the doing

64. 242 U. S. 167.

of such acts does not preclude it from imposing such conditions. The police power is not confined to regulations of public health, morals, safety, and the like. It affects economic as well as social conditions. "It embraces regulations designed to promote public convenience or the general prosperity or welfare."[65] The conditions, to be sure, must be such as fairly fall within the proper scope of the police power, and such as do not violate any rights guaranteed by the federal Constitution, such as those protected by the interstate-commerce clause or by the "privileges and immunities" clauses or the due-process clause, or the clause forbidding a state to deny to any person within its jurisdiction the equal protection of the laws. Undoubtedly a statute forbidding a foreign corporation to enter the state to carry on interstate commerce, without filing a consent to the jurisdiction of the courts of the state as to all causes of action, no matter where or how arising, is unconstitutional.[66]   Similarly, doubtless, a

65. Sligh v. Kirkwood, 237 U. S. 52, 59, 59 L. ed. 835, 35 Sup. Ct. 501 (1915). See also Central Loan & Trust Co. v. Campbell, 173 U. S. 84, 43 L. ed. 623, 19 Sup. Ct. 346 (1899); C. B. & Q. Railway v. Drainage Comm'rs, 200 U. S. 561, 592, 50 L. ed. 596, 26 Sup. Ct. 341 (1906); Bacon v. Walker, 204 U. S. 311, 51 L. ed. 499, 27 Sup. Ct. 289 (1907); Noble State Bank v. Haskell, 219 U. S. 104, 55 L. ed. 112, 31 Sup. Ct. 186 (1911); Eubank v. Richmond, 226 U. S. 137, 57 L. ed. 156, 33 Sup. Ct. 76 (1912). See FREUND, POLICE POWER, §§ 8, 12.

66. Sioux Remedy Co. v. Cope, 235 U. S. 197, 205, 59 L. ed. 193, 35 Sup. Ct. 57 (1914). In that case the court said: "The second [condition], respecting the appointment of a resident agent upon whom process may be served, is

statute forbidding a nonresident to operate his automobile within the state, unless he has consented to submit himself to the jurisdiction of the courts of the state as to all causes of action, whether or not arising out of the operation of the automobile in the state, would be unconstitutional. Similarly, doubtless, a statute providing that nonresidents should not do business within the state without having consented to the jurisdiction of the courts of the state as to all causes of action, no matter where or how arising, would be unconstitutional.

But there would seem to be no objection to a statute which forbids nonresidents to do business within the state without having consented to the jurisdiction of the courts of the state as to all causes of action arising within the state and out of the business carried on within the state. Such a provision seems essentially just. Very clearly provisions allowing creditors to attach the assets employed in the business within the state are

particularly burdensome, because, as the Supreme Court of the state has said, it requires the corporation to subject itself to the jurisdiction of the courts of the state in general as a prerequisite to suing in any of them; that is to say, it withholds the right to sue even in a single instance until the corporation renders itself amenable to suit in all the courts of the state by whosoever chooses to sue it there. If one state can impose such a condition others can, and in that way corporations engaged in interstate commerce can be subjected to great embarrassment and serious hazards in the enforcement of contractual rights directly arising out of and connected with such commerce. As applied to such rights we think the conditions are unreasonable and burdensome, and therefore in conflict with the commerce clause."

desirable and proper, and such provisions are well-nigh universal; but very frequently the business is carried on without the use of any property within the state. In such a case should a creditor of the business be bound to resort to other states to search out and discover the owner of the business? That would seem to be a hardship to the creditor. The words of Mr. Justice Swayne, speaking of the unfairness of refusing a creditor the right to sue a foreign corporation in the state where the corporation was carrying on business and where the cause of action arose, are equally applicable here. "In many instances the cost of the remedy would have largely exceeded the value of its fruits. In suits local in their character, both at law and in equity, there could be no relief. The result would be, to a large extent, immunity from all legal responsibility."[67] On the other hand there is little hardship on the owner of the business if he is required to answer for all claims arising out of the business in the place where the business is carried on. A statute requiring persons carrying on business within the state to consent to service of process upon an agent in actions arising within the state out of the business carried on within the state, would therefore seem to fall within the proper scope of the police power.

If a state has power to forbid a nonresident to do business without having filed a consent to

67. Railroad Co. v. Harris, 12 Wall. (U. S.) 65, 84, 20 L. ed. 354 (1870).

service of process upon his agent, the question arises whether the state has jurisdiction in the absence of such express consent. We have seen that in the case of corporations, on one or the other of three possible theories, the Supreme Court has held that the state may acquire jurisdiction over foreign corporations doing business within the state, as to causes of action therein arising, although no consent was expressly given. How far are these three theories applicable to the case of nonresident individuals? It seems impossible to say that the nonresident is present and "found" within the state; an individual cannot be present except where his physical body is. But it would seem that it is as easy to apply the doctrine of "implied" consent to an individual nonresident, as to a foreign corporation. If the mere fact that a corporation does business in a state constitutes a consent to the conditions which the state may properly and does impose, it is hard to see why the doing of business by an individual is not a consent to the conditions which the state may properly and does impose. The mere fact that the state may not properly impose conditions upon individuals which it may impose upon corporations is immaterial, as long as the conditions it does impose are proper. Furthermore if, according to Judge Hand's theory, a corporation is bound by conditions imposed by the state, not because it has consented to be bound, but because by voluntarily doing business within the state it

is just and proper to hold that it is bound by the
reasonable regulations of that business by the
state. there is no good reason why an individual
should not likewise be bound.

There are several grounds, however, on which it
may be urged that it is possible to reconcile the
decision in *Flexner v. Farson* with the principles
discussed above.

The Kentucky statutes do not make provision
for any form of substituted or constructive service
upon residents in a proceeding *in personam*. In
Kentucky the only form of service upon residents
in such a proceeding is personal service. Does the
provision for service upon the agent of a nonresident doing business within the state discriminate against nonresidents in such a way as to
violate the constitutional provisions as to privileges and immunities? It would seem not. It is
not necessary to put residents and nonresidents
on an exact equality. Nonresidents have by virtue
of their nonresidence a certain advantage over
residents. It is more difficult to find them within
the jurisdiction and to effect personal service upon
them. Since the discrimination merely removes
this advantage, it is not a violation of the constitutional provisions.[68] The case of *Ballard* v.
Hunter [69] is instructive on this point. In that case

68. Guenther v. American Steel Hoop Co., 116 Ky. 580, 591, 76
S. W. 419 (1903). The opposite view was taken in Moredock v.
Kirby, 118 Fed. 180 (C. C., W. D., Ky., 1902), and in Caldwell
v. ___rmour, 1 Pen. (Del.) 545 (1899).

69. 204 U. S. 241, 51 L. ed. 461, 27 Sup. Ct. 261 (1907).

a proceeding *in rem* was brought in Arkansas for
the sale of land in that state for nonpayment of
taxes. Service was made by publication upon the
defendant, a nonresident owner. This service was
in accordance with the statutes of Arkansas,
which required personal service upon resident
owners at least twenty days before the rendition
of the decree of sale, but which provided for constructive service by publication of four weeks
upon nonresident owners. It was contended that
the statute discriminated against nonresident
owners, in violation of the provisions of the
federal Constitution. As to this Mr. Justice
McKenna said:[70] ''We have no doubt of the
power of the state to so discriminate, nor do we
think extended discussion is necessary. Personal
service upon nonresidents is not always within
the state's power. Its process is limited by its
boundaries. Constructive service is at times a
necessary resource.''[71]

70. 204 U. S. 254.

71. See Kane v. New Jersey, stated *supra,* p. 60.

Similarly it is not uncommon to allow attachment of the property of nonresidents only. This is not an unconstitutional discrimination. Campbell v. Morris, 3 H. & McH. (Md.) 535 (1797).
It is not unconstitutional to allow the attachment of property
of a nonresident without requiring the plaintiff to give a bond,
although such a bond is required in the case of attachment of
property of a resident. Central Loan & Trust Co. v. Campbell,
173 U. S. 84, 97, 43 L. ed. 623, 19 Sup. Ct. 346 (1899); Marsh
v. Steele, 9 Neb. 96 (1879). Compare St. Mary's Petroleum Co.
v. West Virginia, 203 U. S. 183, 51 L. ed. 144, 27 Sup. Ct. 132
(1906), in which it was held that a provision for service upon
the state auditor in actions against nonresident domestic corporations and foreign corporations was not unconstitutional, al-

Again, the Kentucky statute makes no distinction between causes of action arising within the state and causes of action arising elsewhere. To the extent to which the Kentucky statute attempts to allow an action for a cause of action not arising within the state, by service of process upon an agent, it is undoubtedly unreasonable and unconstitutional. But it would seem that there is no objection to holding that the statute is severable and that it is valid as to causes of action arising within the state, out of the business carried on within the state. The statutes relating to corporations frequently make no distinction between causes of action arising within the state and those arising elsewhere, and although under *Old Wayne Life Association* v. *McDonough* and *Simon* v. *Southern Railway,* these statutes have been held invalid as to causes of action arising outside the state, they are upheld as to causes of action arising within the state.

There is, however, a ground upon which *Flexner* v. *Farson* may be supported. The Kentucky statute provided for service upon an agent in charge of the business. The person served in *Flexner* v. *Farson* had ceased to be an agent at the time when process was served upon him. Service therefore was not in accordance with the terms of the statute, and hence was insufficient.[72] The decision is

though there was no similar provision as to resident domestic corporations.

72. See People's Tobacco Co. v. American Tobacco Co., 246 U. S. **79,** 62 L. ed. 587, 38 Sup. Ct. 233 (1918).

therefore reconcilable with the principles advocated above; and it is to be hoped that the Supreme Court of the United States will not feel that it is precluded by the decision from holding that a state may validly provide for service of process upon nonresidents doing business within the state, by service upon an agent, in actions arising in the state out of the business carried on within the state.

CHAPTER III

TRIAL BY JURY

In these days when the demand for a more efficient administration of justice is finding a response as never before in the ranks of the legal profession, when a sympathetic and scientific attempt is being made to simplify procedure in the courts of the several states and of the United States, it is important to consider how far the path is blocked by the provisions in the state and federal constitutions guaranteeing the right to trial by jury.[1] Are these provisions a real obstacle in the path of reform? The answer depends on what is meant by trial by jury.

Perhaps the most striking phenomenon in the history of our procedural law is the gradual evolution of the institution of trial by jury. The jury as we know it today is very different from the Frankish and Norman inquisition, out of which our modern jury has been slowly evolved through

1. It is not the purpose of the writer to discuss the right to trial by jury in criminal actions, nor to consider to what kinds of civil actions the constitutional guaranty extends. Nor will any attempt be here made to discuss the much mooted question of the value of the institution of trial by jury in civil cases. For a discussion of this question, see 3 BL. COMM. *379, *385; Second Report of the Common Law Commissioners, 1853; ERLE, THE JURY LAWS; THE FEDERALIST, No. LXXXIII; FORSYTH, HISTORY OF TRIAL BY JURY, chap. 18; Miller, "The System of Trial by Jury," 21 AMER. LAW REV. 859. As to the present English Practice, see R. S. C., Order 36, rules 2-9.

the centuries of its "great and strange career."[2]
It is different from the assizes of Henry II., that
great reformer of procedural law. It is different
from the trial by jury known to Lord Coke and
to the early American colonists who carried to a
new world the principles of English jurisprudence.[3] "To suppose," says Edmund Burke,
"that juries are something innate in the Constitution of Great Britain, that they have jumped, like
Minerva, out of the head of Jove in complete
armor is a weak fancy, supported neither by precedent nor by reason."[4] In England there has
been a wonderfully steady and constant develop-
ment of trial by jury from the Conquest to the
present day. In this country surely it was not, by
the adoption of our constitutions, suddenly con-
gealed in the form in which it happened to exist
at the moment of their adoption. The procedure
of the first half of the seventeenth century or of
the second half of the eighteenth century surely
was not "fastened upon the American jurisprudence like a strait-jacket, only to be unloosed by

2. THAYER, PRELIMINARY TREATISE ON EVIDENCE AT THE COM-
MON LAW, chaps. 2-4.

3. In the seventeenth century the jurors still were expected to
decide on their own knowledge of the facts and not merely upon
the evidence. THAYER, EVIDENCE, 170-74.

In the early colonial legislation we see recognition of the function of jurors as witnesses. "It is very requisite that part of
the jury at least, come from [the neighborhood where the fact
was committed] who by reason of their near acquaintance with
the business may give information of divers circumstances to the
rest of the jury." 2 HENING'S VA. STAT. L. 63.

4. BURKE, WORKS (3 ed.), VII, 115.

constitutional amendment."[5] The common-law practice described so painstakingly by the learned Mr. Tidd surely did not bodily become a part of the organic law of the United States.

The state constitutions usually contain a general provision that "the right to trial by jury shall remain inviolate," or that "the right to trial by jury, as heretofore enjoyed, shall remain inviolate."[6] In the federal and territorial courts the right to trial by jury in civil cases is guaranteed by the Seventh Amendment to the federal constitution which provides that "in suits at common law, where the value in controversy shall exceed twenty dollars, the right of trial by jury shall be preserved, and no fact tried by a jury shall be otherwise reëxamined in any Court of the United States, than according to the rules of the common law." Since the first ten amendments were intended as limitations on the power of the federal government, the Seventh Amendment does not extend to the state courts. It does not require trial by jury in an action brought in the state courts, even though the action is based on a federal statute, and though the statute provides that the action if brought in a state court shall not be removed to a federal court.[7]

5. See Twining v. New Jersey, 211 U. S. 78, 101, 53 L. ed. 97, 29 Sup. Ct. 14 (1909).

6. See a collection of the various constitutional provisions in the Report of the Board of Statutory Consolidation, New York, 1912, 56-82; also in THOMPSON, TRIALS (2 ed.), § 2226.

7. Minn. & St. Louis R. R. Co. v. Bombolis, 241 U. S. 211, 60

Now what is this trial by jury, the right to which was so highly prized by our ancestors as to be put beyond the power of the legislature to abolish? The constitutions do not define it. Its meaning must be ascertained by a resort to history.

Two propositions are fundamental:

First. Whatever was an incident or characteristic of trial by jury in a particular jurisdiction at the time of the adoption of the constitutional guaranty in that jurisdiction is not thereby abolished. In determining what is meant by trial by jury under the Seventh Amendment, inasmuch as the practice was different in the different colonies,[8] the federal courts look to the common law of England rather than to the law of any particular colony; and incidents of trial by jury, known in England at the time of the adoption of the Seventh Amendment, are not done away with by its adoption.[9]

Second. Although the incidents of trial by jury which existed at the time of the adoption of the constitutional guaranty are not thereby

L. ed. 961, 36 Sup. Ct. 595 (1916); St. Louis & San Fran. R. R. Co. v. Brown, 241 U. S. 223, 60 L. ed. 966, 36 Sup. Ct. 602 (1916); Ches. & Ohio Ry. v. Carnahan, 241 U. S. 241, 60 L. ed. 979, 36 Sup. Ct. 594 (1916).

8. THE FEDERALIST, No. LXXXIII; Reinsch, "The English Common Law in the Early American Colonies," 1 SELECT ESSAYS IN ANGLO-AMERICAN LEGAL HISTORY, 367.

9. Thompson v. Utah, 170 U. S. 343, 349, 42 L. ed. 1061, 18 Sup. Ct. 620 (1898); Capital Traction Co. v. Hof, 174 U. S. 1, 43 L. ed. 873, 19 Sup. Ct. 580 (1899); Maxwell v. Dow 176 U. S. 581, 44 L. ed. 597, 20 Sup. Ct. 448, 494 (1900).

abolished, yet those incidents are not necessarily made unalterable. Only those incidents which are regarded as fundamental, as inherent in and of the essence of the system of trial by jury, are placed beyond the reach of the legislature. The question of the constitutionality of any particular modification of the law as to trial by jury resolves itself into a question of what requirements are fundamental and what are unessential, a question which is necessarily, in the last analysis, one of degree. The question, it is submitted, should be approached in a spirit of open-mindedness, of readiness to accept any changes which do not impair the fundamentals of trial by jury. It is a question of substance, not of form.[10] It has, indeed, been contended that no change is admissible unless it can be demonstrated that the change tends necessarily the better to preserve the jury, and that it is not enough that it does not tend

10. ''The Seventh Amendment, indeed, does not attempt to regulate matters of pleading or practice, or to determine in what way issues shall be framed by which questions of fact are to be submitted to a jury. Its aim is not to preserve mere matters of form and procedure but substance of right. This requires that questions of fact in common law actions shall be settled by a jury, and that the court shall not assume directly or indirectly to take from the jury or to itself such prerogative. So long as this substance of right is preserved the procedure by which this result shall be reached is wholly within the discretion of the legislature, and the courts may not set aside any legislative provision in this respect because the form of action—the mere manner in which questions are submitted—is different from that which obtained at the common law.'' Walker v. Southern Pac. R. R., 165 U. S. 593, 596, 41 L. ed. 837, 17 Sup. Ct. 421 (1897).

necessarily to destroy it.[11] This, it is submitted, is not the proper attitude in which to approach the constitutional question. A great chief justice of Massachusetts, speaking of the provision as to trial by jury in the constitution of that common-wealth, wisely said: "I think we are bound to examine it in no nice, criticising spirit, but to take the broadest and most liberal view of it, with a reverential regard to the great objects and pur-poses of its founders."[12]

An examination of the conception of trial by jury in our Anglo-American system shows that certain elements have long been regarded as of its essence.

I. *Number of jurors.* The term "jury," it is said, connotes a body of twelve, no more and no less. Learned judges have indeed sometimes per-mitted themselves to say that Magna Charta guar-anteed the right to trial by twelve jurors.[13] But this is of course inaccurate; the right to trial by a jury of twelve or of any other number was not guaranteed by the Great Charter.[14] At the begin-ning of the thirteenth century twelve was indeed

11. Schofield, "New Trials and the Seventh Amendment," 8 ILL. L. REV. 381. See also Hackett, "Right to Direct a Verdict," 24 YALE L. J. 127.

12. Shaw, C. J., in Comm. v. Anthes, 5 Gray (Mass.), 185, 222 (1855).

13. See Thompson v. Utah, 170 U. S. 343, 349, 42 L. ed. 1061, 18 Sup. Ct. 620 (1898). See also BAC. ABR., tit. Juries; HAWLES, ENGLISHMAN'S RIGHT, 4.

14. MCKECHNIE, MAGNA CHARTA (2 ed.), 134-38, 375-82.

the usual but not the invariable number.[15] But by
the middle of the fourteenth century the requirement of twelve had probably become definitely
fixed. Indeed this number finally came to be regarded with something like superstitious rever-
ence.[16] It is not strange, therefore, to find that
the very first of our state statutes to be held unconstitutional was a New Jersey statute providing
for a jury of six, which, in 1780, was held by the
Supreme Court of that state to violate the constitutional provision that "the inestimable right of
trial by jury shall remain confirmed as a part of
the law of this colony, without repeal forever."[17]
This idea that the requirement of twelve persons
on the jury is of the essence has been frequently

15. THAYER, EVIDENCE, 85.

16. DUNCOMB, TRIALS PER PAIS (8 ed.), 92; THAYER, EVIDENCE,
85-90. The importance of the number is dwelt upon by Lord Coke,
who says: "And it seemeth to me that the law in this case
delighteth herself in the number of 12 . . . and that number
of twelve is much respected in Holy Writ, as 12 apostles, 12
stones, 12 tribes, etc." Co. LITT. 155a. See also GUIDE TO
ENGLISH JURIES, 10; SOMERS, THE SECURITY OF ENGLISHMEN'S
LIVES, 94. These works were well known to the American colonists.
WARREN, HARVARD LAW SCHOOL, I, 126; JEFFERSON, WORKS, V,
102. By the Duke of York's Laws, 1665, it was provided, however, that "no jury shall exceed the number of seven nor be
under six, unless in special cases upon life and death, the justices
shall think fit to appoint twelve." But twelve was the number
fixed in New York by the Charter of Liberties and Privileges in
1683.

17. Holmes v. Walton, 4 AMER. HIST. REV. 456, WAMBAUGH,
CASES ON CONSTITUTIONAL LAW, 21. This case was decided more
than ten years before the adoption of the Seventh Amendment
to the federal Constitution.

affirmed.[18] But in several states the constitutions have been amended so as to permit of juries of less than twelve.[19]

II. *Unanimity*. And next it is held that a unanimous concurrence by the jurors in the verdict is an essential of trial by jury. There is no such requirement in other systems of law than the Anglo-American system. In early times there was no such requirement in the English law. The judges occasionally took the verdict of eleven, and imprisoned or otherwise punished the obstinate twelfth. But in a case in the fourteenth century such a proceeding was severely condemned, and the court refused to render judgment on the verdict, and ordered that a new jury be sum-

18. Thompson v. Utah, 170 U. S. 343, 42 L. ed. 1061, 18 Sup. Ct. 620 (1898); Collins v. State, 88 Ala. 212, 7 So. 260 (1889); Dixon v. Richards, 2 How. (Miss.) 771 (1838); Foster v. Kirby, 31 Mo. 496 (1862); Opinion of the Justices, 41 N. H. 550 (1860); Lovings v. Norfolk, etc. Ry. Co., 47 W. Va. 582, 35 S. E. 962 (1900). But see Froelich v. Express Co., 67 N. C. 1, 8 (1872). See note in 43 L. R. A. 33.

19. Arizona (courts not of record), California, Colorado, Georgia, Idaho (by consent of parties), Illinois (before justices of the peace), Iowa (inferior courts), Minnesota, Missouri (courts not of record), Montana (justices' courts or by consent in other courts), Nebraska (courts inferior to district court), Nevada (by consent of parties), New Jersey (if matter in dispute does not exceed $50), New Mexico (courts inferior to district court), North Dakota (courts not of record), Oklahoma (county courts and courts not of record), South Dakota (courts not of record), Utah (8 in courts of general jurisdiction, 4 in courts of inferior jurisdiction), Virginia (circuit and corporation courts), Washington (courts not of record), West Virginia (justices of the peace), Wyoming.

moned, and the imprisoned juror discharged.[20]
By the middle of the fourteenth century the requirement of unanimity seems to have become definitely established. The orthodox method of procuring unanimity was to starve and freeze and jolt the jurors until they were all of one mind;[21] and finally this gave way to the modern and more amiable substitute of simply tiring them into concurrence. Long before the adoption of our constitutions the requirement of unanimity was regarded as fundamental.[22] It is not unnatural, therefore, that the courts should hold that under a constitution guaranteeing the right to trial by jury it is not competent for the legislature to dispense with the requirement of unanimity.[23] In an

20. Y. B. 41 EDW. III, 31, 36; HALE, PLEAS OF THE CROWN, II, 297; THAYER, EVIDENCE, 88. Originally in the assizes established by Henry II, if the twelve first summoned were ignorant of the fact, they were rejected and others summoned in their place. If the twelve did not agree, others were added to the jury until twelve did agree. This process was called afforcement of the jury. GLANVILL, Bk. II, chaps. 17, 18; FORSYTH, TRIAL BY JURY, 238; THAYER, EVIDENCE, 62.

21. By a New Jersey statute it was expressly provided that the jury "shall be kept together in some convenient private place without meat, drink, fire or lodging until they all agree upon a verdict." ALLINSON'S LAWS, 470. See also 1 HENING'S VA. STAT. L. 303 (1645); 2 Ibid., 73 (1661-62).

22. HALE, HISTORY OF THE COMMON LAW (4 ed.), 293; THAYER, EVIDENCE, 86.

23. American Publishing Co. v. Fisher, 166 U. S. 464, 41 L. ed. 1079, 17 Sup. Ct. 618 (1897); SCOTT, CAS. CIV. PROC. 401; Springville v. Thomas, 166 U. S. 707, 41 L. ed. 1172, 17 Sup. Ct. 717 (1897); Opinion of the Justices, 41 N. H. 550 (1860). See 24 L. R. A. 272. On the policy of requiring unanimity in civil ac-

increasing number of states, however, the constitutions expressly provide for a verdict by less than the whole number of jurors in civil cases.[24]

III. *Impartiality and competence.* There is another fundamental requirement which is clearly of the essence of trial by jury; the jury must be so selected and so constituted as to be an impartial and fairly competent tribunal. Any action, legislative, executive, or judicial, which excludes from the jury all members of a class, deprives a member of that class of the right to trial by jury;[25] indeed, it deprives him of the equal protection of the laws, and of life, liberty, or property without

tions, see WILSON, WORKS (Andrews' ed.), II, 162-210; FORSYTH, TRIAL BY JURY, chap. 11; CLARKE, UNANIMITY IN TRIAL BY JURY; LONGLEY, OBSERVATIONS ON TRIAL BY JURY; Miller, "The System of Trial by Jury," 21 AMER. L. REV. 859, 862; Third Report of Commissioners on Courts of Common Law, 1831, 69-70 (advising that if no unanimous agreement is reached after twelve hours of deliberation a verdict concurred in by nine should be good).

It would have been possible of course to take a broader view of the constitutional requirement. James Wilson, judge and professor of law, in his lectures on law said: "When I speak of juries, I feel no particular predilection for the number twelve. . . . I see no peculiar reasons for confining my view to a unanimous verdict, unless that verdict be a conviction of a crime. . . . When I speak of juries, I mean a convenient number of citizens, selected and impartial, who, on particular occasions, or in particular causes, are vested with discretionary powers to try the truth of facts." WILSON, WORKS (Andrews' ed.), II, 162.

24. Arizona, California, Idaho, Minnesota, Mississippi, Missouri, Montana, Nevada, New Mexico, Ohio, South Dakota, Utah, Washington.

25. Gibbs v. State, 3 Heisk. (Tenn.) 72 (1871).

due process of law.[26]   So also any other provision
which is calculated to allow prejudiced or biased
persons to serve on the jury is a violation of the
right to trial by jury. But where the interest of a
juror is remote or problematical, although sufficient to constitute a ground of exclusion at
common law, it is competent for the legislature to
allow him to serve. Thus a statute is constitutional which allows an inhabitant or taxpayer of
a town or city to be a juror, although the town or
city is a party, and the inhabitant or taxpayer
may thus be remotely interested in the result.[27]
A statute which provides that the mere formation
or expression of an opinion shall not necessarily
be a ground of exclusion is not unconstitutional;[28]
nor a statute providing for struck juries,[29] nor a
statute changing the number of peremptory
challenges allowable,[30] or the number of the jury
panel,[31] or the mode of selecting jurors, provided
the method is fair.[32]

26. Dennis, "Jury Trial and the Federal Constitution," 6
Col. L. Rev. 423.

27. Comm. v. Worcester, 3 Pick. (Mass.) 462 (1826).

28. Stokes v. People, 53 N. Y. 164 (1873).

29. Lommen v. Minneapolis Gaslight Co., 65 Minn. 196, 68 N.
W. 53 (1897).

30. Walter v. People, 32 N. Y. 147 (1865). Nor, it would seem,
is it a denial of the right to trial by jury to abolish peremptory
challenges. Stilson v. United States, 250 U. S. 583, 63 L. ed.
1154, 40 Sup. Ct. 28 (1919).

31. Conyers v. Graham, 81 Ga. 615, 8 S. E. 521 (1888).

32. People v. Harding, 53 Mich. 48, 18 N. W. 555 (1884);
Dowling v. State, 5 Sm. & M. (Miss.) 664 (1846); State v. Slover,

IV. *Province of the jury.* Trial by jury, then, involves a unanimous determination by twelve disinterested and reasonably competent persons. A determination of what? Of such matters only as are properly within the province of the jury. The jury after all has only a limited and special *rôle.* The court also has a part to play.[33] Where, under our constitutions, is to be drawn the line which separates the province of the jury from that of the court? The guiding principle has indeed been laid down at least since the time of Lord Coke. *Ad quaestionem facti non respondent judices, ad quaestionem juris non respondent juratores.*[34] But the limits of this principle have never been exactly fixed; indeed, they have varied from time to time.

At the time when the first permanent settlements were being established in America there was a great deal of popular enthusiasm in England for trial by jury. This enthusiasm was based chiefly on the value of the institution as a bulwark of liberty, as a means of preventing oppression by the Crown. The Stuart judges were exceeding the bounds of decency in their attempts to coerce juries, and the tide of popular

134 Mo. 607, 36 S. W. 50 (1896); People v. Meyer, 162 N. Y. 357, 56 N. E. 758 (1900).

A statute providing that women may act as jurors is not unconstitutional. *Re* Mana, 178 Calif. 213, 172 Pac. 986 (1918).

33. See Capital Traction Co. v. Hof, 174 U. S. 1, 43 L. ed. 873, 19 Sup. Ct. 580 (1899); Opinion of the Justices, 207 Mass. 606, 94 N. E. 558 (1911).

34. Co. LITT. 155b; THAYER, EVIDENCE, 185.

resentment ran strong. There was a rapid fire of eloquent encomiums and panegyrics—I refer to such popular treatises as "The Englishman's Right," "The Guide to English Juries," "The Security of Englishmen's Lives"—which were received with acclaim by the people in England and which soon found their way across the Atlantic.[35] At the time of the English Revolution this feeling was at its height. Since the jury was regarded as a protection against the despotic power of the Crown, popular writers naturally contended that the widest powers belonged to the jury; that they were the sole judges of the law and of the facts; that although the judges might advise them as to the law, yet they had not merely the power but the right to determine for themselves whether the judges' view of the law was correct or not. This doctrine found its most emphatic expression, of course, in criminal suits. In the trial of Colonel Lilburne for treason, in 1649, the doughty defendant uttered a challenge which delighted his fellow countrymen, when he said: "The jury by law are not only judges of fact but of law also, and you who call yourselves judges of the law are no more but Norman intruders, and indeed and in truth, if the jury please, are no more but cyphers to pronounce their verdict." Mr. Justice Jermin in wrathful defense of the bench, replied: "Was there ever such a

---

35. The first-named book was reprinted in America in 1693; the third-named, in 1720. WARREN, HARVARD LAW SCHOOL, I, 126.

damnable blasphemous heresy as this is, to call the judges of the law cyphers?"[36] And even in civil cases the same view found wide popular support. In that popular treatise, "The Security of Englishmen's Lives," Lord Somers said:[37] "As it hath been the law, so it hath always been the custom and practice of these juries, upon all general issues, pleaded in cases civil as well as criminal, to judge both of the law and fact."

Shortly after the English Revolution however a change took place. The direct power of the Crown over the judges ceased when in 1700, by the Act of Settlement,[38] it was provided that they should hold office no longer at the pleasure of the Crown but for life or good behavior. The confidence of the people in the judges increased, and there was a corresponding diminution in the extravagant enthusiasm for wide power in the jury. Burke, that sturdy upholder of liberty, says: "What does a juror say to a judge, when he refuses his opinion upon a question of judicature? 'You are so corrupt, that I should consider myself a partaker of your crime, were I to be guided by your opinion'; or, 'You are so grossly ignorant, that I, fresh from my hounds, from my plough, my counter, or my loom, am fit to direct you in your own profession.' This is an unfitting,

36. VARAX, TRIAL OF COLONEL LILBURNE (2 ed.), 107; 4 How. St. Tr. 1270, 1379.
37. Page 95.
38. 12 & 13 WILL. III, c. 2.

it is a dangerous state of things.''[39] It may safely be said that at the time of the American Revolution the general principle was well established in the English law that ''juries must answer to questions of fact and judges to questions of law. This is the fundamental maxim acknowledged by the constitution.''[40] But, as we shall see, the inadequacy of the methods of keeping the jury within their proper sphere gave rise to certain difficulties.

In the American colonies during the eighteenth century there was a gradually increasing popular enthusiasm for trial by jury and a popular desire strictly to limit the powers of the judges and to give the jury great latitude. The Crown judges were generally and increasingly unpopular. Often, too, they were incompetent; sometimes they were laymen, ignorant of the principles of the law. It was generally contended that even in civil cases the jury had the right as well as the power to decide questions of law as well as of

39. BURKE, WORKS (3 ed.), VII, 119.

40. WYNNE, EUNOMUS, Dialogue III, § 53. See FORSYTH, TRIAL BY JURY, chap 12. See especially Hargrave's note to Co. LITT. 155b. The question of the right of the jury to bring in a general verdict in criminal libel cases gave rise in the latter part of the eighteenth century to a renewal of the controversy as to the respective functions of court and jury. See Woodfall's Case, 20 How. St. Tr. 895 (1770); King v. Dean of St. Asaph, 3 T. R. 428, note; BURKE, WORKS (3 ed.), VII, 105-27; FORSYTH, TRIAL BY JURY, 267-82; WORTHINGTON, POWER OF JURIES. There are provisions as to this in many of the state constitutions. See 33 L. R. A. (N. S.) 207.

fact.[41] But this extreme view, which was largely
the result of a temporary reaction against usur-
pations by corrupt or incompetent or at any rate
unpopular judges, did not by the adoption of the
constitutional guaranty of trial by jury become a
part of our organic law.[42] On the contrary, as we
shall see, our courts have recognized the broad
principle that the constitutional province of the
jury in civil cases is simply the determination of
questions of fact in issue as to which reasonable
men may reach different results; that the constitutional guaranty is not violated by the exercise
of control by the court either (1) in keeping the
jury to the determination of questions of fact, or
(2) in keeping it within the bounds of reason in
determining questions of fact.[43] It is true that at
common law the jury sometimes has the right or
at least the power to do more than this. That is
due, as we shall see, to certain defects in the ma-

41. See a learned note in Quincy's Mass. Rep. 556-72. See also
JEFFERSON, WORKS, III, 235; *Ibid.*, V, 102; WILSON, WORKS
(Andrew's ed.), II, 214-24; SWIFT, SYSTEM OF LAWS, II, 259. In
Georgia v. Brailsford, 3 Dall. (U. S.) 1, 1 L. ed. 483 (1794),
Jay, C. J., so charged the jury in a case tried at the bar of the
Supreme Court.

42. Sparf v. United States, 156 U. S. 51, 39 L. ed. 343, 15
Sup. Ct. 273 (1895); Comm. v. Anthes, 5 Gray (Mass.) 185
(1855); THOMPSON, TRIALS (2 ed.), §§ 940-51, 2132-49. In
the constitution of Georgia of 1777 (§ XLI), however, it was
expressly provided that "the jury shall be judges of law, as
well as of fact, and shall not be allowed to bring in a special
verdict."

43. THAYER, EVIDENCE, 208.

chinery whereby the jury is confined to the exercise of its special office.

What, then, are the methods of controlling the jury? At the outset one is struck by the fact that there is no simple, systematic, adequate method. The methods of controlling the jury grew up in a haphazard sort of way. Most of them grew up at a time when the jurors still had a right to decide upon their own knowledge, as well as upon the evidence, a right which in the eighteenth century became obsolete.[44]

A. *Questions arising on the pleadings.* The concurrence of the jury is not always necessary for the rendition of a judgment in an action at law. No question is presented for the consideration of the jury unless the parties have reached an issue of fact.[45] If the pleadings terminate in a de-

44. 3 BL. COMM. *374.

45. See Willion v. Berkley, 1 Plowd, 223, 230 (1561). In the case of a default or of a demurrer, if the damages are unliquidated, a question of fact as to the amount of damages will arise. Must this be submitted to a jury? At common law damages in such cases would usually be ascertained by a jury summoned on a writ of inquiry and presided over by the sheriff, but that jury was not necessarily composed of twelve persons (DUNCOMB, TRIALS PER PAIS [8 ed.], 93; Co. LITT. 155a, Hargrave's note); or the court might determine the question of the amount of damages without reference to any jury. SELLON, PRACTICE (1 Am. ed.), 347; Watt v. Watt, [1905] A. C. 115, 119. It has been held, therefore, in some cases that the constitutional right to trial by jury does not extend to the question of the *quantum* of damages on default or demurrer. Raymond v. Danbury & Norwalk R. R. Co., Fed. Cas. 11593, 14 Blatchf. 133, 43 Conn. 596 (1877); SCOTT, CAS. CIV. PROC. 547; Hopkins v. Ladd, 35 Ill. 178 (1864); SCOTT,

murrer, an issue of law only is raised, and that
issue is for the determination of the court. This
is the case when the pleading demurred to does
not state facts which constitute a cause of action
or a defence, or when it discloses an affirmative
defence, or when having stated sufficient facts to
constitute a cause of action or defence, it then
unnecessarily states evidence of those facts, which
evidence is insufficient to sustain them.[46] At common law by the use of special pleading, by spread-
ing the facts on the record, a case could sometimes
be kept from the jury. This was indeed the great
purpose of the special traverse. Instead of simply
denying directly, the pleader would allege facts
constituting an argumentative denial, and add a
direct denial. The purpose was to invite a demurrer, in order that the question, whether the
facts alleged in the argumentative denial were
sufficient as a matter of law to meet the other's
case, might be raised on the pleadings and determined by the court, instead of being raised at the
trial, where the jury might or might not follow
the instructions of the judge on the law.[47] So also
the purpose of the substitution of a plea by way
of confession and avoidance for the general issue
by the strange method of making an admission of
a "colorable" right in the plaintiff, was to get

CAS. CIV. PROC. 546. But see Central, etc. R. R. Co. v. Morris,
68 Tex. 49, 3 S. W. 457 (1887). See 20 L. R. A. (N. S.) 1.

46. First Nat. Bank v. St. Croix Boom Corp., 41 Minn. 141,
42 N. W. 861 (1889); SCOTT, CAS. CIV. PROC. 175.

47. STEPHEN, PLEADING, *205.

the facts on the record in order to avoid a jury trial.[48] One of the principal ends aimed at by the common-law commissioners in 1830 in advocating the limitation of the general issue and the extension of special pleading was the severance on the record of the law from the facts.[49] All these things which were incidental to trial by jury at common law are not, of course, forbidden by our constitutions. The law has greatly varied from time to time as to just how much should or may properly be stated in the pleadings. Surely the legislature can constitutionally regulate the rules of pleading so as to require matters to be stated on the record which at common law did not have to be so stated and thus, more fully than at common law, separate on the record questions of law from questions of fact,—just as indeed it may go to the other extreme and provide that the legal elements constituting a cause of action need not be stated, but only such a description of the cause of action as will give to the opposite party notice of the nature of the claim against him.[50]

48. Leyfield's Case, 10 Rep. 88 (1610); STEPHEN, PLEADING, *233; THAYER, EVIDENCE, 232; JENKS, SHORT HISTORY OF ENGLISH LAW, 163.

49. Second Report, 46.

50. The present system of pleading whereby questions of law are supposed to be separated from questions of fact, too often resulted in earlier days in technical decisions, and today, when amendments and pleading over are freely allowed, in delay. The substitution of a system of notice pleading has been urged by Dean Pound in place of the present system. Pound, "Some Principles of Procedural Reform," 4 ILL. L. REV. 388, 491, at

B. *Questions not arising on the pleadings.* When questions of law are not separated on the record from questions of fact, it is a more difficult task to keep separate the respective functions of court and jury. If the pleadings terminate in an issue of fact, various questions of law as well as of fact may arise at the trial. How then may the court confine the jury to its special office?

1. *Instructions to the jury.* The duty of the trial judge is not merely to preside at the trial, to keep order, to determine questions on the admissibility of evidence: it is his duty also to instruct the jury. As far back as the Year Books go we find the court delivering a charge to the jury. The difficulty with this method of controlling the jury is of course that when the facts are doubtful there may be no way of determining whether or not the jury has followed the instructions of the judge on the law. At common law it was clearly proper for the judge not merely to state the law and to sum up the evidence, but also to express an opinion on the questions of fact in issue as long as he leaves to the jury the ultimate determination of the issue, and makes it clear that it is not bound to adopt his opinion as its own. Since the judge had this power at common law, he is not deprived of it merely because the right to trial by jury is guar-

pages 494-97. See also Whittier, "Notice Pleading," 31 HARV. L. REV. 501. If there are really effective means of keeping the jury within their province as to questions not arising on the pleadings, the desirability of raising questions of law on the pleadings is greatly diminished.

anteed by the constitution.[51]   But in many of the
states this power has been expressly taken away
by constitutional or statutory provisions.[52]   It
may well be questioned how far the legislature can
constitutionally curtail in this way the power of
the judge. "Trial by jury, in such a form as that,
is not trial by jury in any historic sense of the
words. It is not the venerated institution which
attracted the praise of Blackstone and of our ancestors, but something novel, modern, and much
less to be respected."[53]

2. *The attaint and motion for a new trial.* If a
verdict has been rendered by a jury on a material
issue of fact, can it be overturned? From the
beginning of the thirteenth century at least, and
in theory, though not in practice, until the nineteenth century, if the verdict was against the evidence or rather false in fact, it could be set aside
by attaint. A new and greater jury could be summoned to examine into the issue tried by the jury,
and if it found that the verdict was false, the verdict would be reversed, and the original jury
severely punished.[54]   Since at that period the

51. Vicksburg, etc. R. R. Co. v. Putnam, 118 U. S. 545, 30 L. ed.
257, 7 Sup. Ct. 1 (1886); United States v. Reading R. R., 123
U. S. 113, 31 L. ed. 138, 8 Sup. Ct. 77 (1887); Lovejoy v. United
States, 128 U. S. 171, 32 L. ed. 389, 9 Sup. Ct. 57 (1888); Simmons v. United States, 142 U. S. 148, 35 L. ed. 968, 12 Sup. Ct.
171 (1891); SCOTT, CAS. CIV. PROC. 358.

52. Sunderland, "The Inefficiency of the American Jury," 13
MICH. L. REV. 302.

53. THAYER, EVIDENCE, 188, note.

54. "An attaint, the greatest punishment they know on this
side death." GUIDE TO ENGLISH JURIES, 4.

jurors might decide on their own knowledge as well as on the evidence, their verdict would not be reversed if supported either by the evidence or by facts not in evidence. This uncouth and barbarous method of controlling the jury was in use in this country in colonial times,[55] and indeed it became so frequent in Massachusetts that a statute had to be passed to prevent its abuse.[56] But gradually both in England and in the American colonies as the idea gained ground that the jurors are to decide merely on the evidence and not on facts known to them, it became obsolete, and a new method of controlling the jury became necessary. In 1655 the first reported decision was rendered holding that the court might order a new trial on the ground that the verdict was against the evidence.[57] This did not necessarily mean that the jurors intentionally went wrong, and did not involve a punishment for them. The granting of new trials on the ground that the verdict was against the evidence or on the ground that the damages awarded were excessive or inadequate soon came into common use in England. In the American colonies new trials were not very frequently granted on these grounds, but they were not unknown.[58] Of

---

55. Quincy's Mass. Rep. 559; 1 R. I. Col. Rec. 200 (1647).

56. 5 Mass. Col. Rec. 449 (1684).

57. Wood v. Gunston, Style, 466; Scott, Cas. Civ. Proc. 464.

58. Quincy's Mass. Rep. 84. Compare the old New England and Georgia practices whereby the losing party was entitled to a new trial as a matter of right. 63 U. Pa. L. Rev. 592, note. See also United States v. 1363 Bags, 2 Sprague, 85 (1863); Bartholomew v. Clark, 1 Conn. 472 (1816).

course this practice is not unconstitutional. Indeed, it has been held on the contrary that a statute denying the court the right to grant a new
trial is unconstitutional.[59] In England the motion was made before the full court in which the
case was pending; and no appeal was allowed
from its decision until the Common Law Procedure Act of 1854.[60] In this country the courts
have upheld the power of the appellate court as
well as of the trial court to order a new trial on
the ground that the verdict is against the evidence
or that the damages are excessive or inadequate.[61]
In some of the cases the question whether such
practice is a violation of the constitutional right
to trial by jury was expressly considered and an-

59. Capital Traction Co. v. Hof, 174 U. S. 1, 43 L. ed. 873, 19
Sup. Ct. 580 (1899); Opinion of the Justices, 207 Mass. 606, 94
N. E. 558 (1911). See Bright v. Eynon, 1 Burr. 390 (1757)
("Trials by jury, in civil causes, could not subsist now without
a power, somewhere, to grant new trials." *Per* Lord Mansfield,
393). See also 3 BL. COMM. *390.

60. Section 35. The motion is now made in the Court of Appeal.
R. S. C., Order 39, rule 1.

61. In a few jurisdictions, however, the rule is otherwise.
Southern Ry. Co. v. Bennett, 233 U. S. 80, 58 L. ed. 860, 34 Sup.
Ct. 566 (1914). See Riddell, "New Trials in Present Practice,"
27 YALE L. J. 353, 361. In Metropolitan R. R. Co. v. Moore, 121
U. S. 558, 573, 30 L. ed. 1022, 7 Sup. Ct. 1334 (1887), Mr.
Justice Matthews, in speaking of the practice of reviewing in an
appellate court the action of the trial court in refusing to grant
a new trial on the ground that the verdict was against the weight
of evidence, said: "Such a practice in the appellate courts of the
United States is perhaps forbidden by the Seventh Amendment."
But this casual doubt seems not well founded.

swered in the negative.[62] The objection to this method of controlling the jury is the delay and expense involved.

At common law if a new trial was ordered, it had to be a new trial as to all the parties and on all the issues. But there is no reason for re-trying the issues as to one party because of an error affecting only another party, or for re-trying one issue because of an error affecting only another issue. Statutes have accordingly provided in some jurisdictions that the new trial shall be confined to the parties as to whom or the issues as to which the verdict is set aside. In some states the same result has been reached without the aid of any statute.[63] This practice is not unconstitutional.[64] Each issue as to each party is determined by a jury; it is not necessary that all the issues should be determined by the same jury.

If a verdict is excessive and the plaintiff is willing to remit the excess and take what the court regards as a fair sum, the court may refuse to grant a new trial. The defendant cannot successfully claim that he has been denied the right to trial by jury. Similarly the defendant may prevent a new trial on the ground that the damages are inadequate by consenting to the entry of a judgment for an adequate amount.[65]

62. Devine v. St. Louis, 257 Mo. 470, 165 S. W. 1014, 51 L. R. A. (N. S.) 860 (1914).

63. Lisbon v. Lyman, 49 N. H. 533 (1870).

64. See Chapter IV, *infra.*

65. See Chapter IV, *infra.*

3. *Demurrer to evidence.* As early as the fifteenth century, this method of withdrawing the case from the jury was employed.[66] After the party having the burden of proof, the proponent, as Professor Wigmore calls him, had introduced all his evidence, the opposing party might demur thereto. If in his demurrer he admitted the truth of the evidence offered by his adversary, the latter was compelled to join in the demurrer. It was not until 1793 that it was held that if the evidence is circumstantial, the demurrant must admit the facts which that evidence tends to prove.[67] The jury who had heard the evidence might be asked to find the amount of damages, but all other questions were withdrawn from them. The difficulty with a demurrer to evidence is that it is a two-edged sword; for if the court is of the opinion that the jury could have found for the proponent, judgment is given for him, whether the court is of the opinion that the jury would have so found or not;[68] and the demurrant waives his right to put in his own evidence or to have a jury decide the issue.[69] It is clear that the constitutional provision as to trial by jury does not preclude a de-

66. THAYER, EVIDENCE, 234.

67. Gibson v. Hunter, 2 H. Bl. 187 (1793); THAYER, EVIDENCE, 235.

68. Cocksedge v. Fanshaw, Doug. 119, 129 (1779); Southern Ry. Co. v. Tyree, 114 Va. 318, 76 S. E. 341 (1902); SCOTT, CAS. CIV. PROC. 303.

69. Galveston, etc. Ry. Co. v. Templeton, 87 Texas, 42, 26 S. W. 1066 (1894); SCOTT, CAS. CIV. PROC. 301.

murrer to evidence.[70] It is a practice long antedating the adoption of our constitutions; and it does not deprive the jury of their proper function.

4. *The special verdict.* At common law if the jurors wished to bring in a general verdict they could do so. They ran a risk in so doing, inasmuch as, if the verdict was wrong, they might be attainted, whether they went wrong on the facts or on the law.[71] And it was a question whether the fact that they had followed the directions of the judge on the law constituted a defence. But it was manifestly unfair to the jurors to subject them to the severe punishment of attaint because of a mistake of law, and therefore they were allowed to bring in a special verdict finding the facts in issue and leaving to the court the determination of the legal effect of those facts. In the American colonies the special verdict was well known.[72] The judge could not refuse to accept a special verdict if it was good and pertinent to the

70. Hopkins v. Railroad, 96 Tenn. 409, 34 S. W. 1029 (1896); SCOTT, CAS. CIV. PROC. 304 and cases cited.

71. Co. LITT. 228a. "Although the jury, if they will take upon them (as Littleton here saith) the knowledge of the law, may give a general verdict, yet it is dangerous for them so to do, for if they do mistake the law, they run into the danger of an attaint; therefore to find the special matter is the safest way where the case is doubtful."

72. CONN. REV. STAT., 1672, 37; 3 MASS. COL. REC. 425; New Jersey Statute of April 23, 1724; New York, Duke of York's Laws, 1665-75. It is said that special verdicts were uncommon in the early history of New England. LECHFORD, PLAIN DEALING, 66. See 3 MASS. COL. REC. 425. In Georgia special verdicts were expressly forbidden by the constitution of 1777, § XLI.

issue.[73] The objection to special verdicts is the technical nicety with which they must be framed. The court cannot take the place of the jury in finding any of the facts in issue necessary to the foundation of the judgment.[74] If the jury finds merely evidence of the facts in issue, the court has not power to draw inferences as to the facts themselves. But if the jury finds facts sufficient to enable the court to enter judgment, but also draws a general conclusion based on an erroneous view of the law, the court may give judgment upon the facts as found and disregard the conclusion of the jury.[75] Not infrequently the judges attempted to compel the jurors to bring in special verdicts, but the jurors fought stoutly against such attempts on the part of the judges and in the end were successful. By statute in many of the states today, however, the court may compel the jury to bring in a special verdict. And in many jurisdictions the court may compel the jury to make special findings of fact in addition to its general verdict; and if those special findings are inconsistent with the general verdict, the court may disregard the general verdict and enter judgment for the opposite party, and need not order a new trial.[76] Such statutes are constitutional. And yet they de-

73. Co. LITT. 228a; COMPLETE JURYMAN, 246

74. COMPLETE JURYMAN, 247.

75. Foster v. Jackson, Hob. 52a; Priddle & Napper's Case, 11 Co. Rep. 8a, 10b; COMPLETE JURYMAN, 252.

76. Walker v. New Mexico, etc. R. R. Co., 165 U. S. 593, 41 L. ed. 837, 17 Sup. Ct. 421 (1897).

cidedly change the common-law rule. They take away from the jury the power to take the law into its own hands by rendering a general verdict on the combined law and facts involved in the issue. They remove the chief prop of the old popular idea that the jury has the right to determine the law.

5. *The special case and reserved point.* Again, the jury might give a general verdict for one party, subject to the opinion of the court *in banc* on a question of law involved, stated in a special case or in a point reserved, drawn up by or under the supervision of the judge.[77] If there was any difference of opinion as to the facts proved, the opinion of the jury was taken and the facts stated in accordance with its opinion. It would seem that the consent of the jury was necessary to this proceeding in the absence of the consent of both parties.[78] If the question was resolved in favor of the party for whom the general verdict was given, judgment would be entered on the verdict for him. If the law was found to be the other way, the verdict would be changed accordingly, and verdict and judgment would be given for the opposite party. If it was so defectively stated that no judgment could be given on it, the court would order a new trial.[79] This practice differed from

77. SMITH, ACTION AT LAW (2 ed.), 113, 129; STEPHEN, PLEADING, *101. See Dublin, etc. Ry. Co. v. Slattery, 3 App. Cas. 1155, 1204-05 (1878).

78. Mead v. Robinson, Barnes Notes (3 ed.) 451; 3 BL. COMM. *378.

79. TIDD, PRACTICE, (9 ed.) 931.

the special verdict in that the question of law did not appear on the record, and therefore the question could not be carried by writ of error to a higher court,[80] whereas a special verdict was entered on the record, and the question of law could be carried up to the higher court on a writ of error. This practice probably goes back to the seventeenth century;[81] it became very common during the eighteenth century.[82] It is therefore clearly constitutional.[83]

6. *Direction of verdict.* When on the evidence there is no question of fact as to which reasonable men might differ, the courts have had no difficulty in saying that the direction of a verdict does not violate the constitutional provision for trial by jury.[84] This method of withdrawing the case from

80. This was changed by the Common Law Procedure Act, 1854, §§ 32, 34.

81. See Allen v. Dundas, 3 T. R. 125, 131 (1789).

82. In the second volume of Wilson's Reports, for example, there are about forty instances of this practice.

83. See Bothwell v. Boston El. Ry. Co., 215 Mass. 467, 102 N. E. 665 (1913); Ann. Cas. 1914D, 275; L. R. A. 1917F, 167; Scott, Cas. Civ. Proc. 341. As to criminal cases, see 4 Ill. L. Rev. 200-01.

84. Improvement Co. v. Munson, 14 Wall. (U. S.) 442, 20 L. ed. 867 (1871); Pleasants v. Fant, 22 Wall. (U. S.) 116, 22 L. ed. 780 (1874); Oscanyan v. Arms Co., 103 U. S. 261, 26 L. ed. 539 (1880); Patton v. Texas, etc. Ry. Co., 179 U. S. 658, 45 L. ed. 361, 21 Sup. Ct. 275 (1901). But if there is a real conflict in the evidence it is unconstitutional to withdraw the case from the jury. Baylies v. Travelers' Ins. Co., 113 U. S. 316, 28 L. ed. 989, 5 Sup. Ct. 494 (1885). In many jurisdictions a verdict may be directed even for the party who has the burden of proof. Herbert v. Butler, 97 U. S. 319, 24 L. ed. 958 (1877); Randall v. Baltimore

the jury is different from a demurrer to evidence. The motion is quite informal and is usually oral. If the motion is denied, the moving party is not precluded from putting in his own evidence and from submitting the issues to the jury. Its operation is also different. On a demurrer to evidence the jury is not called upon to take any further part in the trial unless to determine hypothetically the *quantum* of damages. In the case of a directed verdict the jury is called upon to render the verdict. But the jury has no discretion in the matter. The direction of a verdict is sometimes a cumbersome method of disposing of the case; for a juror may for conscientious or less worthy reasons, refuse to accede to the direction of the court.[85] In a few states this difficulty is avoided by the use of

& Ohio R. R. Co., 109 U. S. 478, 27 L. ed. 1003, 3 Sup. Ct. 322 (1883); Delaware, etc. R. R. Co. v. Converse, 139 U. S. 469, 35 L. ed. 213, 11 Sup. Ct. 569 (1891). See 11 MICH. L. REV. 198. In 1757, Lord Mansfield directed a verdict for the plaintiff who had the burden of proof. Decker v. Pope, 1 Selwyn, Nisi Prius (13 ed.), 91.

85. It has been said that jurors in a civil case refusing to render a verdict in accordance with the direction of the court may be punished for contempt. Cahill v. Chicago, etc. Ry. Co., 74 Fed. 285, 20 C. C. A. 184 (1896); BAC. ABR., tit. Juries, M (2). At common law in civil cases it came to be the view that where an attaint lies, the court cannot punish the jury for refusing to bring a verdict in accordance with the direction of the court. THAYER, EVIDENCE, 165, 166. But this doctrine was established at a time when the jurors were entitled to act on their own knowledge. And of course in criminal cases, where the court is held not to be empowered to direct a verdict of conviction, the jury cannot be punished for refusing to convict. Bushell's Case, Vaughan, 135, 6 How. St. Tr. 999 (1670); THAYER, EVIDENCE, 160-69.

a very simple practice; when on the evidence there is no question of fact as to which reasonable men might differ, the court may dismiss the jury and enter a verdict without the formal concurrence of the jury. It would seem that this practice does not impair the right to trial by jury.[86]

7. *Compulsory nonsuit.* At common law non-suits were wholly voluntary. The plaintiff might absent himself at the time of the rendition of the verdict, and in his absence no verdict could be rendered. The result was that the plaintiff would be nonsuited and the case would end. Inasmuch as the plaintiff was not thereby precluded from bringing a new suit, he was given a great opportunity to harass the defendant by bringing repeated actions against him and becoming nonsuit at the last moment before the jury has rendered its verdict.[87] Statutes have sometimes provided for compulsory nonsuit. A compulsory nonsuit differs from a directed verdict, in that there is

86. Van Ness v. Van Ness, Fed. Cas. No. 16,869 (1846); Cahill v. Chicago, etc. Ry. Co., 74 Fed. 285, 20 C. C. A. 184 (1896); Cloquet Lumber Co. v. Burns, 207 Fed. 40, 124 C. C. A. 600 (1913); Curran v. Stein, 110 Ky. 99, 60 S. W. 839 (1901); Pardee v. Orvis, 103 Pa. 451 (1883). The *dictum* of Harlan, J., in Hodges v. Easton, 106 U. S. 408, 27 L. ed. 169, 1 Sup. Ct. 307 (1882), SCOTT, CAS. CIV. PROC. 430, to the opposite effect is, it is submitted, erroneous.

87. The right has generally been somewhat cut down by statute. In England the plaintiff cannot become nonsuit or discontinue his action if a step has been taken after the defendant has filed his statement of defense. R. S. C., Order 26, rule 1. In this country very generally the plaintiff may become nonsuit at any time until the case is finally submitted to the jury.

not even a formal concurrence on the part of the jury. It differs also in that, like a voluntary non-suit, it does not prejudice the plaintiff's right to bring a new action.[88] Although the compulsory nonsuit was unknown at the time of the adoption of our constitutions, it is nevertheless universally held not to impair the right to trial by jury.[89] It does not take away from the jury any question of disputed fact.

8. *Motion to strike out sham pleading.* If a party interposes a pleading which is clearly false in fact and which is interposed merely for the purpose of delay or vexation he has no right to go to the jury. Such a pleading is called a sham pleading. The opposite party may treat it as a nullity and enter judgment for himself, or he may apply to the court to strike it from the record.[90] In some jurisdictions it has been held, however, that to strike out as sham a negative pleading is to deny the right to trial by jury.[91] But this seems wrong. Although it is a rule of the common law that the

88. Mason v. Kansas City Belt Ry. Co., 226 Mo. 212, 125 S. W. 1128, 26 L. R. A. (N. S.) 914 (1910).

89. Coughran v. Bigelow, 164 U. S. 301, 41 L. ed. 442, 17 Sup. Ct. 117 (1896); Naugatuck R. R. Co. v. Waterbury Button Co., 24 Conn. 468 (1856); Perley v. Little, 3 Me. 97 (1824); Munn v. Pittsburgh, 40 Pa. 364 (1861).

90. See 1 CHITTY, PLEADING (16 Am. ed.), *567; Phillips v. Bruce, 6 M. & Sel. 134 (1817); Merrington v. A'Becket, 3 D. & R. 231 (1823). A statute providing that the defendant must file an affidavit of defense as a condition precedent to trial by jury is constitutional. Fidelity, etc. Co. v. United States, 187 U. S. 315, 47 L. ed. 194, 23 Sup. Ct. 120 (1902).

91. Wayland v. Tysen, 45 N. Y. 281 (1871).

general issue is not to be struck out as sham, because the defendant has a right to put the plaintiff to the proof of his claim in all cases, yet it
would seem that the legislature has the power to
change this rule.   In a New Jersey case [92] the
court said:

> "If, therefore, the plea of the general issue
> is filed when the defendant has no defence,
> it tends only to illegal delay and comes within
> the definition of a sham plea. If it be said
> that if the general issue may be stricken out
> as a sham plea, or regarded by the plaintiff as
> a nullity, the defendant will be deprived of
> a trial by jury, the answer is that the prac-
> tice in this country, as well as in England, of
> striking out false pleas, other than the gen-
> eral issue, whereby the defendant may be de-
> prived of a trial, is well settled. It cannot
> be said that the party is deprived of a trial
> if he has nothing to try."

9. *Motion for judgment notwithstanding the
verdict.* If the pleadings have raised an immaterial issue, and if the jury has brought in a verdict on that issue, it is clear that the court may
arrest the judgment or enter judgment against the
party who obtained the verdict; for since the issue
is immaterial, the verdict is immaterial, and the
court may give judgment on the pleadings. But
suppose that the question arises not on the plead-

92. Walter v. Walker, 35 N. J. L. 262 (1871).

ings but on the evidence. Suppose that a motion is made at the trial for a compulsory nonsuit or the direction of a verdict, and that the court erroneously refuses to grant the motion and the verdict is rendered against the party who made the motion; what is the remedy? At common law the only remedy is a new trial.[93] But why should a new trial be given when the verdict could properly have been given only for the party who lost at the trial? In several jurisdictions statutes have provided that in such a case as this, the trial court or the appellate court may enter judgment in favor of the party for whom the verdict should have been rendered. Is this practice unconstitutional? In the well-known case of *Slocum* v. *New York Life Insurance Company*,[94] the Supreme Court of the United States by a bare majority held that it is. That decision however has met with a great deal of criticism,[95] and the state

93. But see Skeate v. Slaters, 30 T. L. R. 290 (1914); Banbury v. Bank of Montreal, [1918] A. C. 626, 32 HARV. L. REV. 711; Astley v. Garnett, 20 Brit. Col. R. 528 (1914); Dowagiac Mfg. Co. v. Schroeder, 108 Wis. 109, 84 N. W. 14 (1900); SCOTT, CAS. CIV. PROC. 489; Muench v. Heinemann, 119 Wis. 441, 96 N. W. 800 (1903).

94. 228 U. S. 364, 57 L. ed. 879, 33 Sup. Ct. 523 (1913).

95. Thorndike, "Trial by Jury in United States Courts," 26 HARV. L. REV. 732; Thayer, "Judicial Administration," 63 U. PA. L. REV. 585; Rep. Amer. Bar Assoc., 1913, 561. See 32 HARV. L. REV. 711; 33 *ibid.* 246. But see Schofield, "New Trials and the Seventh Amendment," 8 ILL. L. REV. 287, 381, 465 (supporting the Slocum Case on the ground of the second clause of the amendment).

courts have reached the opposite result.[96] On principle the state courts seem clearly right. There is no valid objection to doing after the trial what admittedly might and should have been done at the trial. There is no encroachment upon the proper province of the jury.

10. *Evidence on appeal.* Frequently verdicts and judgments have to be set aside because of the failure to prove some fact at the trial which could have been proved by such clear and incontrovertible evidence that the court would have been justified on such evidence in giving a peremptory instruction to the jury on that point. At common law the practice was to grant a complete new trial. If there has to be a new trial, the new trial should be confined to the consideration of that point alone. But if the point is not one on which a jury could have any doubt, there should be no necessity for submitting it to a jury. The English Rules allow the Court of Appeal to receive "further evidence upon questions of fact, such evidence to be either by oral examination in court, by affidavit or by deposition taken before an examiner or commissioner."[97] The New Jersey Practice Act, 1912, provides that

> "Upon appeal, or on application for a new trial, the court in which the appeal or appli-

96. Bothwell v. Boston El. Ry. Co., 215 Mass. 467, 102 N. E. 665 (1913); SCOTT, CAS. CIV. PROC. 341; Kernan v. St. Paul City Ry. Co., 64 Minn. 312, 67 N. W. 71 (1896); Dalmas v. Kemble, 215 Pa. 410, 64 Atl. 559 (1906).

97. Order 58, rule 4.

cation shall be pending may, in its discretion, take additional evidence by affidavit or deposition, or by reference; provided, that the error complained of is lack of proof of some matter capable of proof by record or other incontrovertible evidence, defective certification, or failure to lay the proper foundation for evidence which can, in fact, without involving some question for a jury, be shown to be competent."[98]

In this practice there is no violation of the constitutional guaranty of trial by jury; no question is withdrawn from the jury upon which the parties have a right to insist upon the opinion of the jury.

Summary. Is the constitutional guaranty of trial by jury an obstacle in the path of procedural reform? It does prevent the determination of questions of fact by less than twelve persons; but that difficulty is one which has been easily removed by an amendment to the constitution when it has been felt desirable, and it has been very generally felt desirable in the case of inferior courts. It does prevent a verdict in which the jurors do not all concur; but this difficulty, if it is a difficulty, is also easily done away with by constitutional amendments when it is felt desirable. It does prevent trial by manifestly partial

98. Section 28. *Cf.* KANSAS CODE OF CIVIL PROCEDURE, § 580. See Rep. Amer. Bar Assoc., 1910, 645; Pound, "Some Principles of Procedural Reform," 4 ILL. L. REV. 338, 491, at page 505. See Chapter V, *infra.*

or clearly incompetent jurors; but that is as it should be. It does prevent the encroachment by the court on the province of the jury, as it prevents the encroachment by the jury on the province of the court; but that is as it should be, provided always that trial by jury is worth preserving in civil cases. But—and this is the fundamental point which the writer has tried to develop—it does not prevent the use of any methods of effecting the division of functions of court and jury.[99] The old methods of enforcing the division which were in use before our constitutions were adopted are clearly not unconstitutional. Nor does it violate our constitutions to supplement or supersede those methods by other methods more readily calculated to effect the division of functions without undue formality or delay. The constitutional guaranty does not stand in the way of the accom-

---

99. In *Ex parte* Peterson, 253 U. S. 300, 309, 64 L. ed. 919, 40 Sup. Ct. 543 (1920), Mr. Justice Brandeis said: "The command of the Seventh Amendment that 'the right of trial by jury shall be preserved' does not require that old forms of practice and procedure be retained. Walker v. New Mexico & Southern Pacific R. R. Co., 165 U. S. 593, 596. Compare Twining v. New Jersey, 211 U. S. 78, 101. It does not prohibit the introduction of new methods for determining what facts are actually in issue, nor does it prohibit the introduction of new rules of evidence. Changes in these may be made. New devices may be used to adapt the ancient institution to present needs and to make of it an efficient instrument in the administration of justice. Indeed, such changes are essential to the preservation of the right. The limitation imposed by the Amendment is merely that enjoyment of the right of trial by jury be not obstructed, and that the ultimate determination of issues of fact by the jury be not interfered with."

plishment of the result, much to be desired, that there shall be no trial by a jury when there is no disputable question of fact to be tried, and no new trial when there is no disputable question of fact left undetermined. If the ancient institution of trial by jury is to survive, as our ancestors intended that it should, it must be capable of adaptation to the needs of the present and of the future. This means that it must be something more than a bulwark against tyranny and corruption: it must be an efficient instrument in the administration of justice.

CHAPTER IV

EXCESSIVE AND INADEQUATE DAMAGES

If an issue of fact is reached in an action at law, the jury may be called upon to determine two questions, namely, that of liability and, if the verdict is for the plaintiff, that of the amount to which he is entitled. If the amount which, if anything, the plaintiff is entitled to recover is liquidated, the jury should be instructed that if it finds for the plaintiff it must find a verdict for the liquidated sum. If the damages are not liquidated, they are assessed by the jury under instructions given by the court as to the principles of law governing the measure of damages.

It may happen that, although a verdict for the plaintiff is proper, yet the amount of damages assessed by the jury is not justified by the law and the evidence. If the court has given erroneous instructions as to the measure of damages, or if evidence as to the amount of damages has been improperly admitted or excluded, the verdict should not stand, provided the error was prejudicial. Under the earlier rule it was enough that the error might have been prejudicial.[1] Today in many jurisdictions a new trial will not be granted on the ground of misdirection or the improper admission or rejection of evidence unless in the opinion of the court some substantial wrong

1. Baron de Rutzen v. Farr, 4 Adol. & El. 53 (1835); SCOTT, CAS. CIV. PROC. 454.

or miscarriage has been occasioned.[2] In some of these jurisdictions the party resisting the new trial has the burden of convincing the court that the error was probably not prejudicial; in others the burden is on the party seeking a new trial to convince the court that the error was probably prejudicial.

Although no erroneous instruction has been given or erroneous ruling made by the court, a new trial will be awarded if on all the evidence it appears that the jury has gone beyond the bounds of reason in assessing the damages. Formerly in such cases the sole remedy was a writ of attaint; but in *Wood* v. *Gunston*,[3] decided in 1655, it was held that a new trial might be granted upon the ground that the damages were excessive. In that case Sergeant Maynard for the plaintiff vigorously argued that "after a verdict the partiality of the jury ought not to be questioned, nor is there any Presidents for it in our Books of the Law, and it would be of dangerous consequence if it should be suffered, and the greatness of the damages given can be no cause for a new tryal." But Glynne, C. J., said that "it is frequent in our Books for the Court to take notice of miscarriages of Juries, and to grant new tryals upon them, and

2. R. S. C. (1883), Order 39, rule 6; FED. JUD. CODE, § 269, as amended 40 STAT. L. 1181 (1919); MASS. L. 1913, c. 716, § 1. For a summary of the statutes on this point see Wheeler, "Procedural Reform in the Federal Courts," 66 U. PA. L. REV. 1, 12. See also WIGMORE, EVIDENCE, § 21.

3. Style, 466; SCOTT, CAS. CIV. PROC. 464.

it is for the people's benefit that it should be so, for a Jury may sometimes by indirect dealings be moved to side with one party and not to be indifferent betwixt them;" and a new trial was ordered accordingly. Since that time new trials have been freely granted upon the ground that the damages awarded are excessive.[4]

In cases where the damages are liquidated it is easy to see that the jury has gone wrong when it assesses the damages at too large an amount. If the damages are unliquidated the problem is not so easy. Nevertheless where the jury is clearly unreasonable, its verdict should not stand. This is true even when the determination of the damages rests on no definite rule but lies largely within the discretion of the jury, as in cases of libel or slander. The problem is like that which arises when the court is asked to set aside a verdict upon the ground that it is against the weight of evidence; the test is not whether the court would have reached the same result as the jury reached, but whether twelve sensible men could reasonably have reached that result.[5] There is no doubt either on principle or on the authorities

4. See TIDD, PRACTICE (9 ed.), 909. For cases involving the question of what amount of damages is excessive, see 4 SEDGWICK, DAMAGES (9 ed.), ch. 58; L. R. A. 1915F, 30.

5. Phillips v. London & S. W. Ry. Co., 4 Q. B. D. 406 (1879); 5 Q. B. D. 78 (1879); 5 C. P. D. 280 (1879); SCOTT, CAS. CIV. PROC. 467; Thurston v. Martin, 5 Mas. (U. S.) 497 (1830); Simmons v. Fish, 210 Mass. 563, 97 N. E. 102, Ann. Cas. 1912D, 588 (1912); Doody v. B. & M. R. R., 77 N. H. 161, 89 Atl. 487 (1914).

that the granting of a new trial upon the ground that the damages awarded are excessive, does not involve any encroachment upon the province of the jury or violate the constitutional right to trial by jury.[6]

Similarly a new trial may be ordered when the damages assessed by the jury are inadequate.[7] This may happen as a result of erroneous rulings or instructions of the court or as a result of mistake or misconduct of the jury. In some states by statute, however, it is provided that a new trial shall not be granted on account of the smallness of the damages awarded in actions for injuries to the person or to reputation, or in other actions if the amount awarded equals the actual pecuniary injury suffered.[8] Such statutes seem unfair to the plaintiff. Indeed it is arguable that they violate the constitutional guaranty of trial by jury in that they deprive the court of the power properly to supervise the conduct of the jury.[9]

6. Smith v. Times Pub. Co., 178 Pa. 481, 36 Atl. 296 (1896). See 51 L. R. A. (N. S.) 860.

If the damages awarded are not unreasonably large, it is a violation of the constitutional guaranty to grant a new trial. Halness v. Anderson, 110 Minn. 204, 124 N. W. 830 (1910).

7. Praed v. Graham, 24 Q. B. D. 53 (1889); SCOTT, CAS. CIV. PROC. 465; Doody v. B. & M. R. R., 77 N. H. 161, 89 Atl. 487, (1914). See 4 SEDGWICK, DAMAGES (9 ed.), §§ 1368-72. At one time it was doubted whether a new trial could be ordered on this ground where the damages are not definite in amount. See TIDD, PRACTICE (9 ed.), 909.

8. See Rossi v. Jewell Jellico Coal Co., 157 Ky. 332, 163 S. W. 220 (1914); Norton v. Lincoln Traction Co., 92 Neb. 649, 138 N. W. 1132 (1912) (statute later repealed).

9. Hughey v. Sullivan, 80 Fed. 72 (1897). See Yazoo, etc. R. R.

Partial new trials. At common law a verdict was regarded as indivisible. A new trial could not be granted as to some of the parties and not as to others, or as to some of the issues and not as to others, although the ground for granting the new trial affected only some of the parties or issues.[10] In *Parker* v. *Godin*,[11] an action of trover was brought for various articles including certain plate. The jury found a verdict for the defendant which as to the plate, though not as to the other articles, was against the evidence. It was held that a new trial must be granted as to all the articles, the court holding that this was not unjust to the defendant "for if the merits as to those other things were with defendant, it would be found for him as to them." So when a new trial was granted on the ground that the damages awarded were excessive or inadequate, the new trial was not confined to the question of damages, but the question of liability was also tried over again.

This narrow rule Chief Justice Doe of New Hampshire refused to follow in the case of *Lisbon* v. *Lyman*,[12] in which he delivered an illuminating and exhaustive opinion. In that case the learned

Co. v. Wallace, 90 Miss. 609, 43 So. 469 (1907); Capital Traction Co. v. Hof, 174 U. S. 1, 43 L. ed. 873, 19 Sup. Ct. 580 (1899); Opinion of the Justices, 207 Mass. 606, 94 N. E. 846 (1911).

10. Hodges v. Easton, 106 U. S. 408, 27 L. ed. 169, 1 Sup. Ct. 307 (1882); SCOTT, CAS. CIV. PROC. 430. See TIDD, PRACTICE (9 ed.), 911; 29 CYC. 732.

11. 2 Strange, 813 (1729); SCOTT, CAS. CIV. PROC. 479.

12. 49 N. H. 553, 583 (1870).

Chief Justice laid down "the general principle that when an error has happened in a trial, the party prejudiced by it has a right to the correction of the error, but has not a right to a new trial if the error can be otherwise corrected;" and he further said: "The general principle of the correction of errors which occur in judicial proceedings, preserves, as far as possible, what is good, and destroys only what is erroneous when the latter can be severed from the former." This principle was accepted in some other states [13] and has been adopted by rule of court in England and by statute in a number of states.[14] Thus the New Jersey Practice Act, 1912,[15] provides that "When a new trial is ordered because the damages are excessive or inadequate, and for no other reason, the verdict shall be set aside only in respect of damages, and shall stand good in all other respects."

There are cases, however, in which it would be improper to confine the new trial to the question of damages. The issues in a case may be so interdependent that it would be misleading to the jury upon the new trial to confine them to the consideration of some only of those issues. In *Nor-*

13. San Diego L. & T. Co. v. Neale, 78 Calif. 63, 20 Pac. 372 (1888); Scott, Cas. Civ. Proc. 477; Boyd v. Brown, 17 Pick. (Mass.) 453, 461 (1835); Taylor v. Winsor, 30 R. I. 44, 73 Atl. 388 (1909). See 29 Cyc. 732.

14. See R. S. C. (1883), Order 29, rules 6 and 7; Mass. L. 1913, c. 716, § 1.

15. Rule 73. See Young v. Society, etc. of Verona, 91 N. J. L. 310, 102 Atl. 358 (1917).

folk Southern Railroad Company v. *Ferebee,*[16] an action was brought in a court of North Carolina on the federal Employers' Liability Act. The court gave an erroneous charge as to the amount of damages. The jury found specially that the defendant railroad was negligent and that the plaintiff was not guilty of contributory negligence. The Supreme Court of the state granted a new trial, confining the new trial to the question of damages. Accordingly, evidence of contributory negligence offered at the subsequent trial was refused; and this ruling was upheld by the Supreme Court of the state, and by the Supreme Court of the United States. Mr. Justice Lamar, however, took occasion to utter a warning against the granting of partial new trials unless the issues are separable.[17] He said:

"Damages and contributory negligence are so blended and interwoven, and the conduct of the plaintiff at the time of the accident is so important a matter in the assessment of damages, that the instances would be rare in which it would be proper to submit to a jury the question of damages without also permitting them to consider the conduct of the plaintiff at the time of the injury.

"But this record, in connection with the special-finding first verdict, shows that in

16. 238 U. S. 269, 59 L. ed. 1298, 35 Sup. Ct. 780 (1915).

17. Schmidt v. Posner, 130 Ia. 347, 106 N. W. 760 (1906); Merony v. McIntyre, 82 N. C. 103 (1880).

this case the two matters were in fact separable, so that the splitting up the issues and granting a partial new trial did not in this particular instance operate to deprive the defendant of a Federal right. For it appears that Ferebee had nothing to do with the loss of the steps and was not guilty of contributory negligence in failing to see that they were missing. His conduct at the time of his fall could not, therefore, affect the amount of the verdict so that it was possible, on the second trial, to award damages without considering the conduct of the plaintiff or retrying the question of contributory negligence.''

Furthermore, the fact that the jury has awarded excessive damages may show a bias or prejudice against the defendant, or other improper motive, of such a character that the determination of the question of liability as well as the question of damages was probably affected thereby. In that case of course a new trial should not be confined to the question of damages and it is necessary to have a trial by a new jury of all the issues.[18] But the mere fact that the jury awards excessive damages is not enough to impeach the whole verdict. The excessive amount of the verdict does not necessarily show bias or prejudice, or other improper motive; and even though bias or prejudice

18. McNamara v. McNamara, 108 Wis. 613, 84 N. W. 901 (1901).

or other improper motive is shown, the determination of the question of liability was not necessarily affected thereby.

When the jury has awarded inadequate damages, a new trial may be granted upon the question of damages alone.[19] But it may be improper to confine the new trial to the question of damages. Thus the inadequacy of the damages awarded may be the result of an improper compromise on the question of liability. In *Simmons* v. *Fish*,[20] the plaintiff, a boy under twenty-one years of age, sued the defendant for negligence resulting in the loss of one of his eyes. The evidence as to the loss of the eye was undisputed, but there was a real dispute on the question of the defendant's negligence. The jury found a verdict for the plaintiff for $200. The plaintiff moved that the verdict as to damages be set aside and a new trial ordered on the question of damages only. The motion was allowed by the trial court. The Supreme Judicial Court held that the sum of $200 was obviously inadequate, and that its inadequacy showed that the verdict must have been "the result, not of justifiable concession of views, but of improper compromise of the vital principles which should have controlled the decision;" that the whole verdict was therefore in-

19. Scott v. Yazoo, etc. R. R. Co., 103 Miss. 522, 60 So. 215, 108 Miss. 871, 67 So. 491, L. R. A. 1915E, 240 (1914) ; Clark v. New York, etc., R. R. Co., 33 R. I. 83, 80 Atl. 406, Ann. Cas. 1913B, 356 (1911).

20. 210 Mass. 563, 97 N. E. 102, Ann. Cas. 1912D, 588 (1912).

valid, and that the new trial should not be confined to the question of damages.[21]   Indeed it would seem that the defendant as well as the plaintiff was entitled to insist upon a new trial.

It would seem clear that there is nothing unconstitutional in confining a new trial to the parties as to whom or the issues as to which the verdict is invalid.   Each issue as to each party is determined by a jury; it is not necessary that all the issues as to all the parties should be determined by the same jury.   Chief Justice Rugg, of the Supreme Judicial Court of Massachusetts, has thus justified the granting of partial new trials:

> "The guiding principle is that, although a verdict ought not to stand which is tainted with illegality, there ought to be but one fair trial upon any issue, and that parties ought not to be compelled to try anew a question once disposed of by a decision against which no illegality can be shown.   Thus the parties and the Commonwealth have been saved the expense, annoyance and delay of a retrial of issues once settled by a trial as to which no reversible error appears."[22]

Accordingly it has been held that the granting of

21. See Murray v. Krenz, 94 Conn. 503, 109 Atl. 859 (1920); F. & B. Livery Co. v. Indianapolis, etc. Co., 124 N. E. 493 (Ind App., 1919); Waucantuck Mills v. Magee Carpet Co., 225 Mass. 31, 113 N. E. 573 (1916); Doody v. B. & M. R. R., 77 N. H. 161, 89 Atl. 487 (1914). See 29 YALE L. JOUR. 458.

22. Simmons v. Fish, 210 Mass. 563, 97 N. E. 102, Ann. Cas. 1912D, 588 (1912).

partial new trials does not violate the constitutional guaranties as to trial by jury.[23]

The opposite result, however, was reached by the federal Circuit Court of Appeals, in the third circuit, in a recent case.[24] In that case, in pursuance of the provisions of the New Jersey Practice Act, the federal District Court ordered a new trial on the ground that the damages assessed were inadequate, the new trial to be confined to the determination of the amount of damages. It was held by the Circuit Court of Appeals that this order involved a violation of the Seventh Amendment to the federal Constitution. The court showed by copious illustrations that such restricted new trials were not permissible at common law, and assumed that therefore they involved a violation of the constitutional guaranty of trial by jury. This assumption was not justified; as has been shown, it is not every change in trial practice that violates the constitutional guaranty. Changes are permissible which do not undermine the fundamental principles of trial by jury. As long as each issue in the case is determined by a jury, there is no infringing of the province of the jury. It is to be hoped and con-

23. Farrar v. Wheeler, 145 Fed. 482, 75 C. C. A. 386 (1906); Calaf v. Fernandez, 239 Fed. 795, 152 C. C. A. 581 (1917); Original, etc. Mine v. Mining Co., 254 Fed. 630 (1918); Opinion of the Justices, 207 Mass. 606, 94 N. E. 846 (1911); Yazoo, etc. R. R. Co. v. Scott, 108 Miss. 871, 67 So. 491, L. R. A. 1915E, 240 (1914).

24. McKeon v. Central Stamping Co., 264 Fed. 385 (1920). See 34 HARV. L. REV. 71; 69 U. PA. L. REV. 71.

fidently expected that the Supreme Court of the United States will overrule this decision. The granting of partial new trials prevents unnecessary expense and delay; and to hold that they are precluded by the constitutional provisions as to trial by jury would be most unfortunate.

Avoiding a new trial. It is clear then that a new trial may be granted on the ground that the jury has awarded excessive or inadequate damages; and according to the modern view the new trial may be confined to the question of damages, provided that question is not inseparably interwoven with the other issues, and provided the other issues are not also tainted. But it is possible to avoid a new trial altogether by a remittitur of the excess or by payment of the deficiency.

1. *Permitting the plaintiff to remit the excess.* The court, either the trial court or an appellate court,[25] may deny a new trial although the damages awarded were excessive, if the plaintiff is willing to submit to a deduction of the excess.

This is clear where the amount of the excess is definite, or can be computed with exactness. In the recent English case of *Lionel Barber & Co.* v. *Deutsche Bank*,[26] the plaintiffs brought an action for libel. The court erroneously instructed the jury that a certain item of £460 might be included in the damages to be awarded. The jury found a

25. In some states the jurisdiction of the highest appellate court is confined to questions of law. See 4 SEDGWICK, DAMAGES (9 ed.), § 1332.

26. [1919] A. C. 304.

verdict for the plaintiffs, and assessed their damages at £3,000 and judgment was entered accordingly. Ultimately upon appeal to the House of Lords, the plaintiffs consented at the bar of the House to a deduction of £460. It was held (Lord Atkinson and Lord Phillimore dissenting), that the defendant was not entitled to a new trial, but that judgment should be entered for the plaintiffs for £2,540.[27]

So also where the jury find for the plaintiff for an amount greater than that laid in the *ad damnum* clause of the plaintiff's declaration, if the plaintiff is willing to remit the excess, judgment may be entered for the amount laid in the *ad damnum* clause.[28] But the court may allow an amendment of the *ad damnum* clause, and either allow judgment to be entered for the amount of the verdict or order a new trial.[29]

In many of the cases in which the damages awarded by the jury are excessive, the amount of the excess cannot be exactly determined; all that can be said is that the jury have fixed upon an amount unreasonably large. Even in such cases it is held in a great majority of the states that it is proper to deny the defendant's motion for a

27. Williams v. Hanna, 105 Kans. 540, 185 Pac. 17 (1919); 29 Cyc. 1020; Dec. Dig., New Trial, § 162.

28. Pickwood v. Wright, 1 H. Bl. 642 (1791); Scott, Cas. Civ. Proc. 529; Labahn Brick Co. v. Hecht, 169 Ill. App. 447 (1912); Scott, Cas. Civ. Proc. 530.

29. See Taylor v. Jones, 42 N. H. 25 (1860); Scott, Cas. Civ. Proc. 531.

new trial if the plaintiff is willing to remit so much of the damages awarded as to leave a balance which is not in itself excessive.[30] This practice, however, was rejected by the House of Lords in *Watt* v. *Watt*.[31] In that case the plaintiff brought an action for libel and the jury found a verdict for him for £5,000. The Court of Appeal, on the ground that the damages awarded were excessive, made an order for a new trial unless the plaintiff should consent to a reduction of the

30. Gila Valley, etc. Ry. Co. v. Hall, 232 U. S. 94, 58 L. ed. 521, 34 Sup. Ct. 229 (1914); SCOTT, CAS. CIV. PROC. 473; Bothe v. True, 103 Kans. 562, 175 Pac. 395 (1918); Smith v. Martin, 93 Vt. 111, 106 Atl. 666 (1919).

If after the remittitur the balance is still excessive, the appellate court will reverse the judgment and order a new trial unless the plaintiff submits to a further deduction. De Puy v. Kann, 32 N. Y. App. D. 638, 53 N. Y. S. 1103 (1898). See Stemmerman v. Nassau El. R. R. Co., 36 N. Y. App. D. 218, 56 N. Y. S. 730 (1899).

In Tomljanovich v. Victor Amer. Fuel Co., 227 Fed. 951 (1915), it was said that the court in giving the plaintiff an option to remit, should fix such amount as to leave a balance as large as a jury could reasonably award. In Wisconsin, on the other hand, the court fixes such an amount as to leave a balance as small as a jury could reasonably award. Beach v. Bird & Wells Lumber Co., 135 Wis. 550, 116 N. W. 245 (1908), discussed *infra*. The proper rule would seem to be that if the plaintiff consents, the defendant cannot object if the amount fixed by the court is not more than the amount which the jury actually awarded and also not more than the maximum amount a jury might reasonably award. The smaller the sum fixed the less likely the plaintiff is to consent. The problem is different when the question is one of compelling the plaintiff to accept less than the jury has awarded. See page 131, *infra*.

31. [1905] A. C. 115, overruling Belt v. Lawes, 12 Q. B. D. 356 (1884).

damages to £1,500. The House of Lords reversed this order, and ordered a new trial without giving the plaintiff an option of remitting part of the damages. It was admitted that the order of the Court of Appeal was in accordance with an established practice; and Lord Davey admitted that the practice was convenient and that such an order would in most cases do substantial justice and save expense; but it was thought that the practice involved an encroachment upon the province of the jury. But it seems that there is no such encroachment. The plaintiff cannot object, for he is precluded by his consent.[32] The defendant should not be allowed to object, for he is not compelled to pay more than the jury might properly award and did in fact award. The court is not substituting its judgment for that of the jury; it is not deciding what amount the plaintiff ought to recover; it is merely deciding that a part of what the jury awarded was not an excessive amount.

Accordingly the Supreme Court of the United States and many of the state courts have held that this practice does not violate the constitutional guaranty of the right to trial by jury;[33] nor does

32. Koenigsberger v. Richmond Silver Min. Co., 158 U. S. 41, 39 L. ed. 889, 15 Sup. Ct. 751 (1895); Colorado City v. Liafe, 28 Colo. 468, 65 Pac. 630 (1901).

33. Arkansas Val. L. & C. Co. v. Mann, 130 U. S. 69, 32 L. ed. 854, 9 Sup. Ct. 458 (1889); Koenigsberger v. Richmond Silver Min. Co., 158 U. S. 41, 39 L. ed. 889, 15 Sup. Ct. 751 (1895); Gila Valley, etc. Ry. Co. v. Hall, 232 U. S. 94, 58 L. ed. 521, 34

it violate the other provision of the Seventh Amendment to the federal Constitution that "no fact tried by a jury shall be otherwise re-examined in any court of the United States than according to the rules of the common law." In *Arkansas Valley Land & Cattle Co.* v. *Mann*,[34] Mr. Justice Harlan said:

> "It cannot be disputed that the court is within the limits of its authority when it sets aside the verdict of the jury and grants a new trial where the damages are palpably or outrageously excessive. . . . But, in considering whether a new trial should be granted upon that ground, the court necessarily determines, in its own mind, whether a verdict for a given amount would be liable to the objection that it was excessive. The authority of the court to determine whether the damages are excessive implies authority to determine when they are not of that character. To indicate, before passing upon the motion for a new trial, its opinion that the damages are excessive, and to require a plaintiff to submit to a new trial, unless, by remitting a part of the verdict, he removes that objection, certainly does not deprive the defendant of any right, or give *him* any cause

Sup. Ct. 229 (1914); SCOTT, CAS. CIV. PROC. 473; Henderson v. Dreyfus, 191 Pac. 442 (N. Mex., 1919). See 29 CYC. 1022; DEC. DIG., New Trial, § 162 (3).

34. 130 U. S. 69, 74, 32 L. ed. 854, 9 Sup. Ct. 458 (1889).

for complaint. Notwithstanding such remission, it is still open to him to show, in the court which tried the case, that the plaintiff was not entitled to a verdict in any sum, and to insist either in that court or in the appellate court, that such errors of law were committed as entitled him to have a new trial of the whole case.''

It is true that in some cases it may appear that the jury reached its verdict as a result of passion or prejudice or other improper motive which probably influenced it not merely in assessing the damages but also in deciding the issues. In such cases, of course, the defendant may insist upon a new trial, and the new trial should not be confined to the question of damages.[35] But the mere fact that the damages are excessive does not evince an improper motive.[36] It is held in many states that the fact that excessive damages have been awarded as a result of passion or prejudice or other improper motive is not necessarily enough to impeach the whole verdict, or even to taint that part of the verdict which awards damages, so far as it is not excessive; but on this there is a diversity of opinion.[37]

[35]. Milford, etc. Co. v. B. & M. R. R. Co., 107 Atl. 313 (N. H., 1919); McNamara v. McNamara, 108 Wis. 613, 84 N. W. 901 (1901).

[36]. Detzur v. B. Stroh Brewing Co., 119 Mich. 282, 77 N. W. 948 (1899); SCOTT, CAS. CIV. PROC. 469. See ANN. CAS. 1912C, 509.

[37]. Trow v. Village of White Bear, 78 Minn. 432, 80 N. W.

Where the court has made an erroneous ruling on the admission or exclusion of evidence as to the amount of damages, or has given an erroneous charge as to the measure of damages, it may be that it is impossible to say how much the jury would have awarded if no such error had been made. In such a case it would seem that a new trial upon the question of damages is necessary, unless the plaintiff is willing to accept the lowest amount which a jury could reasonably have awarded, if it had been uninfluenced by evidence which was improperly admitted, or if it had considered evidence which was improperly excluded, or if it had been properly instructed on the law.[38] Unless such a minimum can be determined and is acceptable to the plaintiff, a new trial must be had upon the question of damages.[39] It is not permissible for the court to refuse to grant a new trial merely because the plaintiff is willing to accept an amount fixed by the court which is not in itself excessive.[40] That would be to substitute the opinion of the court for that of the jury.

An interesting question was raised in *Podgorski* v. *Kerwin*,[41] recently decided in Minnesota. In

1117 (1899); SCOTT, CAS. CIV. PROC. 471. See Henderson v. Dreyfus, 191 Pac. 442 (N. Mex., 1919); 29 CYC. 1023; ANN. CAS. 1912C, 509.

38. Triangle Lumber Co. v. Acree, 112 Ark. 534, 166 S. W. 958 (1914); Smith v. Martin, 93 Vt. 111, 106 Atl. 666 (1919).

39. Smith v. Dukes, 5 Minn. 373 (1861).

40. Jayne v. Loder, 149 Fed. 21, 78 C. C. A. 653 (1906).

41. 179 N. W. 679 (1920); criticised 21 COL. L. REV. 390; 5 MINN. L. REV. 236.

that case the plaintiff brought an action for personal injuries and obtained a verdict for $7,000. Thereafter the defendant moved for a new trial upon the ground of newly-discovered evidence. This new evidence bore upon the amount of damages only, and tended to show that the damages awarded were excessive. The court ordered that a new trial should be granted unless the plaintiff should consent to a reduction of the verdict to $5,000. The plaintiff did consent, and the defendant appealed from the order. The Supreme Court (two justices dissenting) held that the order should be affirmed. It is submitted, however, that it was improper to allow the plaintiff to remit a part of the damages. The defendant never had his day in court with all the evidence which he was entitled to put before the jury. If the jury had had before it the newly-discovered evidence, it might not have awarded as much as $5,000. The plaintiff was therefore allowed to recover more than any jury might have given him upon all the evidence now available. It would seem therefore that the court should have granted a new trial upon the question of damages. If the newly-discovered evidence could not have affected the result to a greater extent than $2,000, then indeed the allowing of the remittitur would have been proper.[42]

2. *Permitting the defendant to pay the de-*

42. Tyler v. North Amer. T. & T. Co., 24 Wash. 252, 64 Pac. 162 (1901).

ficiency. Where the damages are inadequate it would seem that there is no objection to allowing the defendant to avoid a new trial if he is willing to pay such an amount as is not inadequate. The defendant cannot object, for he is bound by his consent. The plaintiff cannot object to the refusal to grant a new trial since he is getting an amount which is not inadequate and which is at least as much as the jury gave him.

This seems clear enough where the proper amount is definite or can be fixed by computation. Thus in *Carr* v. *Miner*,[43] the jury awarded the plaintiff a certain sum with interest at six per cent. Under the law the plaintiff, if entitled to recover, was entitled to interest at ten per cent. Upon motion of the plaintiff for a new trial upon the ground that the amount awarded was inadequate, the trial court intimated that it would grant a new trial unless the defendant would consent to pay interest at the rate of ten per cent. The defendant did so consent, and the motion was overruled, and judgment given for the plaintiff for the increased amount. The Supreme Court held that the judgment should be affirmed.[44]

Even when the amount cannot be exactly fixed,

43. 42 Ill. 179 (1866).

44. See also Marsh v. Kendall, 65 Kans. 48, 68 Pac. 1070 (1902). *Cf.* Anderson v. Jenkins, 99 Ga. 299, 25 S. E. 648 (1895).

If an action is brought upon a promissory note and the jury finds for the plaintiff without saying for how much, the court may enter judgment for the plaintiff for the amount of the note. Betts v. Butler, 1 Idaho, 185 (1868); SCOTT, CAS. CIV. PROC. 524.

it would seem that the plaintiff should not be entitled to insist upon a new trial if the defendant is willing to pay an amount which is not in itself inadequate, and which is even more than the jury in fact awarded. This question was raised in the recent case of *Gaffney* v. *Illingsworth*.[45] In that case the plaintiff brought an action for damages for personal injury caused by the negligence of the defendant, and obtained a verdict of $190.25. Both the plaintiff and defendant obtained rules to show cause why a new trial should not be granted. The court discharged the defendant's rule and made an order granting the plaintiff a new trial as to damages only, but with a proviso that if the defendant should pay $480.50 within ten days, the plaintiff's rule should be discharged. The defendant did not make the payment, and the plaintiff's rule was made absolute. The defendant appealed. It was held by the Court of Errors and Appeals that the action of the trial court was proper. Walker, C., said:

> "The power of the court in granting a new trial upon the ground that the damages are *excessive*, upon terms that a new trial shall be had unless the plaintiff will accept a certain sum named, less than that awarded by a verdict, is too well established to be questioned. It would seem to follow, by parity of reasoning, that when a new trial is granted because the damages are inadequate, the court

45. 90 N. J. L. 490, 101 Atl. 243 (1917).

may impose like terms, that is, terms to the effect that if the defeated party will pay a certain sum, greater than that awarded by the verdict, the rule will be discharged; subject, doubtless, to the power of an appellate court to vacate any such terms when they appear to be an abuse of discretion.'"[46]

If, however, the inadequacy of the damages awarded indicates an improper compromise by the jury, as in the case of *Simmons* v. *Fish,* which was discussed above, then the whole verdict is vitiated and either party is entitled to insist upon a new trial not merely of the question of damages, but of all the issues in the case. But if there is a minimum amount admitted by the defendant to be due, and a compromise on the question whether more is due, the plaintiff may prevent a new trial by consenting to accept the minimum amount. In *Blume* v. *Ronan,*[47] the plaintiff sued to recover $470, the alleged price of certain cattle sold by him to the defendants. The defendants in their answer alleged that the purchase price was $414. On the trial the court directed the jury to render a verdict either for $470 or for $414, with interest. After deliberating for eleven hours, the jury found a verdict for $442 and interest, and a ver-

---

46. Marsh v. Minneapolis Brewing Co., 92 Minn. 182, 99 N. W. 630 (1904); Richards v. Sandford, 2 E. D. Smith (N. Y.) 349 (1854). See also Belt v. Lawes, 12 Q. B. D. 356 (1884) (*semble*), overruled by Watt v. Watt, [1905] A. C. 115.

47. 141 Minn. 234, 169 N. W. 701 (1918).

dict was entered for this amount. The Supreme Court held that the jury had evidently compromised by splitting the difference between the amount claimed by the plaintiff and the amount admitted by the defendant to be due, and held that a new trial should be granted unless the plaintiff should consent to accept $414 and interest. Similarly of course the defendant might prevent a new trial if he should consent to pay $470 and interest.

If the inadequacy of the verdict is due to an erroneous instruction or a misunderstanding by the jury of such a character that it is impossible to know what the jury would have awarded if it had received and understood proper instructions, a new trial cannot be prevented by the defendant's consent to pay a reasonable amount fixed by the court. In *Lorf* v. *City of Detroit*,[48] the plaintiff, a married woman, sued to recover damages for personal injuries. The testimony on behalf of the plaintiff tended to show negligence on the part of the defendant, and injuries of a somewhat serious character. The defendant's evidence tended to show that the plaintiff and her witnesses exaggerated the seriousness of her injuries. The jury found a verdict for the plaintiff in the amount of six cents. The plaintiff moved for a new trial on the ground that the damages were inadequate. The trial court ordered that a new trial be granted unless the defendant should consent to pay $100. The defendant did so consent, and judgment was

48. 145 Mich. 265, 108 N. W. 661 (1906).

entered for the plaintiff for $100. The plaintiff appealed, and the judgment was reversed. It was held that it was erroneous to compel the plaintiff to accept $100. The decision seems sound; for the plaintiff might have recovered more than $100 if the jury had awarded substantial damages as it should have done.[49] It would seem on principle, however, that a new trial need not be ordered if the defendant were willing to pay the maximum amount a jury could properly have awarded.

3. *Compelling the plaintiff to remit the excess.* Can the plaintiff ever be compelled to accept less than the jury gave him? It would seem that if the amount to which the plaintiff is entitled is liquidated, there is no objection to compelling him to remit the excess. It is true that he is not receiving all that the jury wished to give him, but he is receiving all that he is entitled to receive under the law and the evidence. It may be objected, however, that the court is authorizing the entry of a judgment which in part is contrary to the verdict. Is that objection well taken?

49. Where a verdict for the defendant was against the evidence, it was held that the court may not refuse to order a new trial although the defendant consented to pay a reasonable amount fixed by the court. Goldsmith v. Detroit J. & C. Ry., 165 Mich. 177, 130 N. W. 647 (1911); Stanton v. Foley, 168 Mich. 453, 134 N. W. 466 (1912).

In Ford v. Minneapolis St. Ry. Co., 98 Minn. 96, 107 N. W. 817 (1906), it was held that the *defendant* can not object to an order requiring a new trial unless the defendant consents to pay a sum fixed by the court instead of a nominal sum awarded by the jury.

In the well known case of *Slocum* v. *New York Life Insurance Co.*,[50] it was held by the Supreme Court of the United States that where upon the evidence the trial court should have directed a verdict for one party, but the jury finds a verdict for the other party contrary to the evidence, the constitutional guaranty of trial by jury makes it improper to order the entry of judgment notwithstanding the verdict. Fortunately this decision is not followed in the state courts.[51] How far does the decision in the Slocum case make it improper in the federal courts to give a judgment without the consent of the plaintiff for an amount less than the jury has awarded when the amount awarded is greater than is by law allowed?

In the first place it is clear that where it appears upon the face of the record (that is upon the pleadings and verdict) that the amount awarded is excessive, it does not violate the constitutional guaranty of trial by jury for the court, even without the plaintiff's consent, to give judgment for an amount which is as great as is by law

---

50. 228 U. S. 364, 57 L. ed. 879, 33 Sup. Ct. 523 (1913).

51. Bothwell v. Boston El. Ry. Co., 215 Mass. 467, 102 N. E. 665 (1913); Scott, Cas. Civ. Proc. 341; Kernan v. St. Paul City Ry. Co., 64 Minn. 312, 67 N. W. 71 (1896).

At common law a judgment notwithstanding the verdict could be entered only for a party who appeared upon the pleadings entitled to judgment. By statute, however, and in a few states without a statute, it is permissible to enter judgment notwithstanding the verdict for one party, if the court should have directed a verdict for the opposite party. See 32 Harv. L. Rev. 711; 33 Harv. L. Rev. 246. See page 103, *supra*.

allowable, although the jury has awarded a greater amount. The practice of giving judgment for the party appearing on the record to be entitled thereto, notwithstanding a verdict for the opposite party, is old and well established, and its constitutionality was admitted in the Slocum case. In *Insurance Company* v. *Piaggio*,[52] the plaintiff brought suit upon a policy of insurance on a vessel. The jury gave a verdict awarding the whole amount of the policy with interest, and in addition $5,000 for damages, and judgment was entered accordingly. The Supreme Court held that the sum of $5,000 damages should be disallowed, and remanded the case with a direction to enter a verdict for the plaintiff for the residue. Both the fact that the damages were excessive and the exact amount of the excess appeared upon the face of the record.[53]

If the fact and the amount of the excess do not appear upon the face of the record (the pleadings and verdict), but are shown by the rulings or charge of the judge at the trial, or by the evidence, it has been held that where the amount of the excess is definitely calculable the amount of the excess may be disallowed even against the plaintiff's objection, and judgment given for the balance

52. 16 Wall. (U. S.) 378, 21 L. ed. 358 (1872).

53. See also New York, etc. R. R. Co. v. Estill, 147 U. S. 591, 37 L. ed. 292, 13 Sup. Ct. 444 (1893). The same result has been reached where the correct amount appears from special findings of the jury. Kansas City, etc. Ry. Co. v. Turley, 71 Kans. 256, 80 Pac. 605 (1905).

without the necessity for a new trial.[54] It has been
held, however, by a federal District Court, that
under the decision of the Supreme Court in the
Slocum case, this practice is improper in the federal courts, and that a new trial, on the question
of damages at least, is necessary.[55] It may be
hoped, however, that the Supreme Court will not
extend the decision in the Slocum case so as to
apply it where the judgment is only in part op-
posed to the verdict of the jury.

Where the amount of the excess cannot be exactly determined, can the plaintiff be compelled to
remit any part of the amount awarded in the verdict? In several cases a negative answer has been
given to this question. Thus in *Kennon* v. *Gil-
mer*,[56] the plaintiff brought suit in a court of the
territory of Montana to recover for personal injuries. The jury returned a verdict for the plaintiff assessing his damages at the "sum of $20,000
for general damages, and also the sum of $750 for
medical expenses and surgical operations." The
defendants moved for a new trial on the ground
that the damages were excessive. The motion was
denied and judgment was entered on the verdict.
The defendants appealed to the Supreme Court
of the territory, which ordered the judgment to be
reduced to the sum of $10,750, and affirmed it for

54. American Nat. Bank v. Williams, 101 Fed. 943, 42 C. C.
A. 101 (1900); Tootle v. Coleman, 107 Fed. 41, 46 C. C. A. 132
(1901).
55. Original, etc. Mine v. Mining Co., 254 Fed. 630 (1918).
56. 131 U. S. 22, 33 L. ed. 110, 9 Sup. Ct. 696 (1889).

this amount. Upon writ of error sued out by both parties, it was held by the Supreme Court of the United States that the territorial Supreme Court had no power without the plaintiff's consent to reduce the amount awarded by the jury, and that both parties were prejudiced by the order of the territorial court. The decision seems clearly correct.[57] The court is not empowered to substitute its judgment on the question of damages for that of the jury. The plaintiff is entitled to recover any amount a jury may award him provided the amount is not unreasonably large. The amount fixed by the court was not the largest amount which a jury might reasonably have awarded to the plaintiff. The plaintiff was justified in objecting to receiving an amount which was less than the jury actually gave him and which was less than a jury might reasonably give him.

In Wisconsin in a series of cases [58] the Supreme Court has worked out a method of dealing with cases in which the jury has awarded excessive damages where the damages are not definitely calculable. In *Beach* v. *Bird & Wells Lumber Co.*,[59]

---

57. Brown v. McLeish, 71 Iowa, 381, 32 N. W. 385 (1887); SCOTT, CAS. CIV. PROC. 534; Isley v. Bridge Co., 143 N. C. 51, 55 S. E. 416 (1906); Atchison, etc. Ry. Co. v. Cogswell, 23 Okl. 181, 99 Pac. 923 (1909); SCOTT, CAS. CIV. PROC. 475.

In Louisiana where there is no constitutional guaranty of trial by jury in civil cases, the opposite result has been reached. Peyton v. Texas, etc. Ry. Co., 41 La. Ann. 861, 6 So. 690 (1889).

58. See Hanna v. Chicago, etc. Ry. Co., 156 Wis. 626, 146 N. W. 878 (1914), and cases there cited.

59. 135 Wis. 550, 558, 116 N. W. 245 (1908).

the plaintiff sued for personal injuries and the jury awarded him a verdict for $20,000. The trial court took the view that $9,000 was the maximum amount and $5,000 was the minimum which an impartial jury could probably find, and gave the defendant the option to pay $9,000 without the plaintiff's consent, and gave the plaintiff the option to take judgment for $5,000 without the defendant's consent,[60] and ordered that a new trial should be granted if neither chose to exercise his option. The court stated its practice as follows:

> "The court is not authorized to determine what amount of damages the plaintiff shall recover, thus substituting his judgment for that of the jury. But the court is to determine the maximum and minimum amounts that an impartial and unprejudiced jury would probably name, as no two juries, fair and impartial and unprejudiced, would arrive at the same amount. The question is, what would be the smallest amount that any such jury might assess and what the largest amount that any other such jury might honestly assess, and the only way suggested for solving this question is by ascertaining what such juries have done in similar cases and what amounts have been held to be excessively large or small. When these two limits have been arrived at,

60. It would seem that the court might properly give the plaintiff the option of taking more than the minimum amount which a jury might award. See note 30, *supra.*

reasonable doubts being resolved in favor of making the minimum small and the maximum large, the court then gives the defendant the option of consenting to judgment against him for the larger amount, and if he does not so elect the option is then given to the plaintiff to take judgment for the smaller amount, and in the event of neither option being exercised the verdict is set aside and a new trial awarded.''

It would seem that there is nothing unconstitutional in this practice. Although the plaintiff is compelled to forego a part of what the jury awarded to him, he is allowed the maximum amount which on the law and the evidence any jury could properly award to him.[61]

4. *Compelling the defendant to pay the deficiency.* Can the defendant be compelled to pay more than the jury has awarded, where the amount awarded is inadequate? An affirmative answer seems clearly proper where the amount which should be added is definite.

In *Matthews* v. *New York Central, etc., Railroad,*[62] it was held that where owing to an erroneous instruction the jury omitted one item of damage which should have been included, and the

61. In Howard v. Bank of Metropolis, 115 N. Y. App. D. 326, 100 N. Y. S. 1003 (1906), it was held that when the jury gave substantial damages, although on the law and the evidence the plaintiff was entitled only to nominal damages, the court could not order judgment to be entered for nominal damages.

62. 231 Mass. 10, 120 N. E. 185 (1918).

amount of damages awarded by the jury in their general verdict was therefore inadequate, but where the amount due on the omitted item was definitely fixed by answers of the jury to special questions, the court might add the omitted item to the amount awarded in the general verdict, and give judgment accordingly.[63]

In *Schweitzer* v. *Connor*,[64] the plaintiff sued the defendant for cutting and carrying away timber. The trespass was clearly proved. The timber had been manufactured into lumber. It was admitted at the trial that the amount of timber cut was 147,000 feet, and that the value of the logs was $5 for 1,000 feet, or $735 in all; but that the value of the lumber was from $8 to $12 per 1,000 feet, or from $1,176 to $1,764. By statute the plaintiff was entitled to the value of the manufactured lumber, and the court so charged. The jury returned a verdict for $735. Upon the plaintiff's motion, the court increased the verdict to $1,176. The Supreme Court of Wisconsin upheld the order, Cole, C. J., saying:

"It is the duty of the jury to respond as to the facts, and of the court as to the law. This is a maxim of our jurisprudence. So the court, on demurrer to evidence or pleadings, on special verdicts, in granting nonsuits and

63. The same result has been reached when the jury failed to award interest. Alloway v. Nashville, 88 Tenn. 510 (1890). But see Gourdin v. Read, 10 Rich. L. (S. C.) 217 (1857).

64. 57 Wis. 177, 14 N. W. 922 (1883).

in setting aside verdicts, exercises this power, applies the law to the admitted facts, and determines the controversy. Now, when the value and quantity of the lumber manufactured from the logs was admitted, there was really nothing for the jury to ascertain, no fact to be found. As we have said, the court might have directed the jury to return a verdict for the plaintiff for $1,176 damages, and the defendant could have taken no valid exception to such a direction. What was done amounted in substance to the same thing. The jury evidently made a mistake in not following the instruction of the court as to the rule of damages. But upon the admitted facts we are inclined to think the court had power to increase the verdict so as to give the statutory rule.'"[65]

Can the defendant be compelled to pay more than the jury has awarded in cases where the damages are not definite? In Louisiana, where there is no constitutional guaranty of trial by jury in civil actions, it has been repeatedly held that the court may do this; it has been so held even in actions for personal injuries,[66] and in actions for slander.[67] In the latter part of the seventeenth

65. See Hurst v. Webster Mfg. Co., 128 Wis. 342, 107 N. W. 666 (1906). But see Buck v. Little, 24 Miss. 463 (1852); Scott, Cas. Civ. Proc. 534. For conflicting decisions, see 25 L. R. A. (N. S.) 314.

66. Burvant v. Wolfe, 126 La. 787, 52 So. 1025 (1910).

67. Mequet v. Silverman, 52 La. Ann. 1369, 27 So. 885 (1900);

century it was held that in cases of personal injury, where the injury amounted to mayhem, the court might *super visum vulneris* increase the amount of damages when the amount found by the jury appeared to the court inadequate. This peculiar practice seems inconsistent with any logical theory of the function of the jury; it became obsolete in England long before our constitutions were adopted, and has been repudiated in this country.[68]

It would seem clear that the court has no power to substitute its finding as to the amount of damages to which the plaintiff is entitled for the finding of the jury.[69] It would seem on principle, however, that it might be possible where the jury have found a verdict objectionable solely on the ground that the damages awarded were inadequate, to compel the defendant to pay the minimum amount which a reasonable jury could award on the law and the evidence. No decision has been found, however, in which, where the amount of damages is not definite, such a practice has been employed.

Summary. The whole problem in dealing with questions of excessive or inadequate damages is one of isolating the cause of the excess or deficiency. Whenever it is possible to isolate the error, to show the limits of its effect, the part of

Simpson v. Robinson, 104 La. 180, 28 So. 908 (1900) (nominal verdict increased to $500).

68. McCoy v. Lemon, 11 Rich. L. (S. C.) 165 (1856).

69 Empire Fuel Co. v. Lyons, 257 Fed. 890, 169 C. C. A. 40 (1919).

the verdict unaffected by it should be retained, and only such part of the verdict should be set aside as appears to be affected by it.

If a new trial is granted it should be confined to the question of damages, unless the error affected the determination of the issues. It does affect the determination of the issues when the questions of liability and of damages are interdependent. So also it affects the determination of the issues when the ground for holding the damages excessive is bias or prejudice of such a character as to permeate the whole verdict. Similarly, when the damages awarded are inadequate, this fact may show an improper compromise by the jurors on the question of liability. It would seem, however, that it should not be presumed, in the absence of special circumstances, that the whole verdict is vitiated. The party moving for a new trial should have the burden of showing that the whole verdict is so affected.

It is not necessary to grant a new trial if the ground for granting a new trial is removed.

(1) If the jury awards excessive damages and the plaintiff is willing to remit the excess, no new trial should be necessary, unless the rest of the verdict was in some way tainted. This is so whether the amount of the excess is definite or not; but where it is definite it is easier to show that the rest of the verdict was not tainted.

(2) Similarly, when the jury awards inadequate damages, no new trial should be necessary if the

defendant is willing to pay a sum which is not inadequate, unless the rest of the verdict is in some way tainted. This is so whether the amount of the deficiency is definite or not; but where it is definite it is easier to show that the rest of the verdict was not tainted.

(3) Moreover, when the damages awarded are excessive, but the rest of the verdict is in no way tainted, it should be possible to compel the plaintiff to remit the excess, provided he receives all that any jury could properly award him upon the law and the evidence. This is so whether the amount of the excess is definite or not; but if it is definite it is easier to show that he is receiving all that he is entitled to receive. Even if it is indefinite, however, the plaintiff should not be allowed to complain if he receives the maximum amount which a jury could award him upon the law and the evidence.

(4) Similarly, when the jury awards inadequate damages, but the rest of the verdict is in no way tainted, it should be possible to compel the defendant to pay an adequate amount. This is so whether the amount is definite or not; but where the amount is definite it is easier to show that the defendant is paying no more than he is bound to pay. Even if the amount is indefinite, however, the defendant should not be allowed to object if he is compelled to pay no more than the minimum amount to which the plaintiff is entitled on the law and the evidence.

CHAPTER V

AMENDMENTS AND JEOFAILS

It is astonishing how irretrievably fatal was the effect of a mistake in any step in an action at law, in the period when the common-law system of procedure was reaching its maturity. Mistakes made by the clerks in recording judicial proceedings were equally fatal, until Parliament intervened and in a series of statutes of amendments and jeofails gave a moderate measure of relief.[1] With respect to mistakes made by the parties, Parliament was slower to give relief. Until 1585 a defect even of form could be taken advantage of not merely by a general demurrer, but after verdict by a motion in arrest of judgment or in the upper court on a writ of error.[2] Moreover the courts were extraordinarily reluctant to allow the parties to retrieve their mistakes by amendment. In the days of the year-books it was quite different. The pleadings were oral statements made by counsel in open court. If either counsel made a mistake in stating a cause of action or defence nothing was simpler than to make a new and more accurate statement when attention was called to the mistake.[3] When however in the course of time written pleadings were introduced, the courts took a sterner attitude. Even Blackstone, to whom

1. See the statutes cited in STEPHEN, PLEADING, *106 note.
2. STEPHEN, PLEADING, *106.
3. STEPHEN, PLEADING, *80; BOLLAND, THE YEAR BOOKS.

the common-law procedure appeared almost the perfection of wisdom, complains of the refusal of the common-law judges to give the parties permission to amend their pleadings.[4]

The most important of the early statutes of amendments and jeofails is the Statute 27 Eliz. c. 5,[5] enacted in 1585. This statute provides:

> "That from henceforth, after demurrer joined and entered in any action or suit in any court of record within this realm, the judges shall proceed and give judgment according as the very right of the cause of the matter in law shall appear unto them, without regarding any imperfection, defect, or want of form in any writ, return, plaint, declaration, or other pleading, process, or course of proceeding whatsoever, except those only which the party demurring shall specially and particularly set down and express together with his demurrer; and that no judgment to be given shall be reversed by any writ of error, for any such imperfection, defect, or want of form as is aforesaid, except such only as is before excepted."

In other words the statute provides that defects of form can be taken advantage of only by special demurrer. It does not provide that defects of form shall not be fatal to the cause of the

4. 3 BL. COMM. *407-410.
5. Section 1. See SCOTT, CAS. CIV. PROC. 198.

party guilty of them; but it provides that one who wishes to take advantage of such defects must act promptly and openly. It is an important reform, but according to our modern notions a very moderate one. Lord Hobart, who succeeded Lord Coke as Chief Justice of the Court of Common Pleas, referring to the statute, has quaintly observed:

> "Now the moderation of this statute is such, that it doth not utterly reject form; for that were a dishonour to the law, and to make it, in effect, no art; but requires only that it be discovered, and not used as a secret snare to entrap."[6]

The fear of dishonoring the law of pleading by making it no art, has led to the retention of many a rule preventing the determination of causes upon their merits, and serving no useful purpose other than to give to the law of pleading the appearance of artistic symmetry.

The line between defects of form and defects of substance is not an easy one to draw. It has sometimes been said that substance has to do with the matter pleaded, and that form has to do with the manner of pleading. This statement is not very helpful, however, for the distinction is in the last analysis one of degree rather than of kind. A pleading for example may be somewhat too in-

6. Heard v. Baskervile, Hob. 232 (1612).

definite, and so bad in form;[7] or it may be so very indefinite as to fail to state a cause of action or defence, and hence to be bad in substance.[8] Many defects which were once regarded as defects of substance are today regarded as mere defects of form. The omission of the formal words *vi et armis* and *contra pacem regis* was held to be a defect of substance until a statute passed in the reign of Queen Anne provided otherwise.[9]

It was not until the enactment of the Common Law Procedure Act [10] in 1852 that it was provided that defects of form should no longer be open even to a special demurrer. In the United States in a few jurisdictions it is still possible for one party to obtain a judgment on the ground of a defect of form of which the other party has been guilty. In most of the states, however, such defects cannot be taken advantage of by demurrer. If a defect is such as to cause embarrassment to the opposite party, the latter may move to have the defect corrected, but he is not entitled to judgment on account of the defect.

As to defects of substance the law after as before the Statute of Elizabeth was that such defects may be taken advantage of by general demurrer,

7. Central R. R. Co. v. Van Horn, 38 N. J. L. 133 (1875); Scott, Cas. Civ. Proc. 201.

8. Moore v. Hobbs, 79 N. C. 535 (1878); Scott, Cas. Civ. Proc. 171.

9. Stat. 4 Anne c. 16, § 1.

10. Stat. 15 & 16 Vict. c. 76, § 51, providing that ''no pleading shall be deemed insufficient for any defect which could heretofore only be objected to by special demurrer.''

motion in arrest of judgment or writ of error. Even at common law, however, a defect though one of substance may be cured or aided by subsequent proceedings.

Thus if a plaintiff fails to allege in his declaration some essential matter, the defect is cured if the defendant in his plea supplies the missing matter. In the case of *Brooke* v. *Brooke*,[11] decided in the King's Bench in 1664, the plaintiff sued the defendant in trespass for taking a hook, without alleging in his declaration that the hook was in his possession. The defendant pleaded a justification for taking the hook, adding the words "wherefore he took the said hook out of the hands of the plaintiff." After verdict for the plaintiff, the defendant moved in arrest of judgment on the ground that the declaration was insufficient. The court held however that the defect was cured by the defendant's plea, and gave judgment for the plaintiff. A declaration may be aided by allegations in a plea although the plea is filed after the Statute of Limitations has run.[12] Similarly a defective plea may be aided by an admission in the replication.[13] But if the plaintiff states one cause of action in his declaration he cannot recover on a

11. 1 Sid. 184 (1664); SCOTT, CAS. CIV. PROC. 192. See Bate v. Graham, 11 N. Y. 237 (1854); CHITTY, PLEADING (16 Am. ed.), 703; DEC. DIG., Pleading, §§ 401-403.

12. Vickery v. New London Northern R. R. Co., 87 Conn. 634, 89 Atl. 277 (1914).

13. United States v. Morris, 10 Wheat. (U. S.) 246 (1825).

different cause of action admitted by the defendant in the plea.[14]

There is some question whether a defective pleading filed by one party may be aided by allegations in his own subsequent pleading. In *Covey* v. *Henry*,[15] the plaintiff in his petition omitted an essential allegation, which he inserted in his reply. The defendant demurred to the reply. It was held that the demurrer should be sustained; that the defective petition could not be aided by the allegation in the reply, because the allegation was not material to the reply and was not therefore admitted by the defendant's demurrer. In several recent cases, however, a more liberal view has prevailed and the opposite result has been reached.[16] It is not permissible at any rate for the plaintiff to supply a new cause of action in his replication, for that would be a departure.[17]

Defects in pleadings may be cured by verdict. The most common example of this is the case in

14. Marsh v. Bulteel, 5 B. & A. 507 (1822); SCOTT, CAS. CIV. PROC. 194. But see 32 HARV. L. REV. 166.

15. 71 Neb. 118, 98 N. W. 434 (1904). See also Kearney County Bank v. Zimmerman, 5 Neb. (Unof.) 556, 99 N. W. 524 (1904).

16. Marine Trust Co. v. St. James A. M. E. Church, 85 N. J. L. 272, 88 Atl. 1075 (1913); Auxier v. Auxier, 181 Ky. 614, 205 S. W. 684 (1918). See 33 HARV. L. REV. 244; DEC. DIG., Pleading, § 401.

17. A departure, though ground for general demurrer, is cured by verdict. Burdick v. Kenyon, 20 R. I. 498, 40 Atl. 99 (1898). See Plummer, Perry & Co. v. Rohman, 61 Neb. 61, 84 N. W. 600 (1900), holding that advantage of the defect may be taken at the trial.

which one of the material allegations in the plaintiff's declaration or complaint is expressed with too great generality. If the allegation is so general that it amounts to a conclusion of law, the defect will be one of substance which can be taken advantage of by a general demurrer or under the Codes by a demurrer upon the ground of the failure to state a cause of action. If, however, the defendant pleads the general issue or a general denial and a verdict is found for the plaintiff, the defect is cured.[18] No advantage can be taken of the defect in the trial court by a motion in arrest of judgment or in the upper court on a writ of error. It will be presumed that under the instructions of the judge the jury must have found specific facts sufficient to support the general allegation.

Until the verdict is rendered, however, the defect is not cured. It would seem therefore that on a demurrer later in the line of pleadings, or by motion in arrest of judgment after a default, advantage may be taken of the defect.[19] At common law, however, there was no way of attacking the pleadings at the trial. It was too late to demur, and a motion in arrest of judgment could not be

18. Baker v. Warner, 231 U. S. 588, 58 L. ed. 384, 34 Sup. Ct. 175 (1913); Chicago & Alton R. R. Co. v. Clausen, 173 Ill. 100, 50 N. E. 680 (1898); Scott, Cas. Civ. Proc. 500; Dec. Dig., Pleading, §§ 431-437.

19. Dunn v. Sullivan, 23 R. I. 605, 51 Atl. 203 (1902). In some jurisdictions the defect is cured by failure to demur. 3 Whittier, Cas. Com. L. Pleading, 566 note.

made until after the verdict. The reason for this was that at common law the duty of the judge at the trial was only to try issues raised by the pleadings. It was not his duty to determine the sufficiency of the pleadings. The determination of such matters was for the full bench at Westminster in term time, and not for the single judge on circuit in vacation. Hence at common law although the defect of too great generality was not cured until verdict, there was no method of taking advantage of the defect after issue was joined. Today a party may move at the trial for judgment on the pleadings.[20] But it is usually held that the defect of stating a cause of action or defence in too general terms is waived by going to trial without objection, although on strict logic the defect would not be cured until verdict, unless the plaintiff asked for and obtained leave to amend his declaration or complaint.[21]

If a necessary allegation is totally omitted by

20. Humboldt Min. Co. v. American, etc. Co., 62 Fed. 356, 10 C. C. A. 415 (1894) ; Scott, Cas. Civ. Proc. 516; Tooker v. Arnoux, 76 N. Y. 397 (1879). But see Littlefield v. Maine Central R. R. Co., 104 Me. 126, 71 Atl. 657 (1908). In some states the proper method of taking advantage at the trial of a defect in the pleadings is by a motion to exclude all evidence or a motion for a nonsuit or directed verdict. Murphy v. Russell, 202 Mass. 480, 89 N. E. 107 (1909) ; Scott, Cas. Civ. Proc. 517; Rothe v. Rothe, 31 Wis. 570 (1872) ; Dec. Dig., Pleading, § 428.

21. See Goucher v. City of Sioux City, 115 Iowa 639, 89 N. W. 24 (1902) ; Cronan v. City of Woburn, 185 Mass. 91, 70 N. E. 38 (1904) ; Williams v. Raper, 67 Mich. 427, 34 N. W. 890 (1887) ; Dec. Dig., Pleading, § 406 (7).

In Folsom v. Brawn, 25 N. H. 114 (1852), it was held that the

the plaintiff from his declaration and the defendant interposes a general denial, the defect will not be cured by verdict.[22] It will be presumed that the jury merely found on the issues actually raised. There is no reason to presume that they found the existence of any facts not in issue. If, however, the defendant should specifically deny the missing matter and the parties should go to trial as though an apt issue had been framed, the defect will be cured by verdict.[23] Here the record shows that the jury must have found the missing matter. But according to the strictly logical view the defect is not cured until the verdict is rendered; and if at the trial the defendant moves for judgment on the pleadings, judgment will be given for the defendant,[24] unless the plaintiff asks for and obtains leave to amend his declaration or complaint.[25] In some jurisdictions, however, a more liberal view is taken and the specific denial itself has been held to cure the defect.[26] And at com-

defect, although not waived by going to trial, was cured by the admission of evidence without objection.

22. Baker v. Sherman, 73 Vt. 26, 50 Atl. 633 (1901) ; SCOTT, CAS. CIV. PROC. 495.

23. Bruce v. Beall, 100 Tenn. 573, 47 S. W. 204 (1898) ; SCOTT, CAS. CIV. PROC. 504. See Loan & Trust Savings Bank v. Stoddard, 2 Neb. (Unof.) 486, 89 N. W. 301 (1902) ; SCOTT, CAS. CIV. PROC. 253.

24. Scofield v. Whitelegge, 49 N. Y. 259 (1872) ; Tooker v. Arnoux, 76 N. Y. 397 (1879).

25. National Bank v. Rogers, 166 N. Y. 380, 59 N. E. 922 (1901).

26. Grace v. Nesbitt, 109 Mo. 9, 18 S. W. 1118 (1891). See DEC. DIG., Pleading, § 403.

mon law, as has been stated, there was no method of attacking the pleadings at the trial.

In Massachusetts by the Practice Act of 1851 it is provided "that no motion in arrest of judgment for any cause existing before verdict shall be allowed in any case where a verdict has been rendered, unless the same affects the jurisdiction of the court."[27] Thus, although the failure to state a cause of action may be taken advantage of by demurrer, or at the trial by a motion to direct a verdict, a verdict cures even this defect.[28]

At common law nonjoinder and misjoinder of parties appearing on the face of the declaration, being defects of substance, are grounds for demurrer, motion in arrest of judgment or writ of error.[29] Under the Codes, however, such defects can be taken advantage of only by demurrer, pointing out the defect; by failing to demur, the defendant waives the defect.[30] In England and a few states which have adopted modern Practice Acts, nonjoinder and misjoinder of parties are no longer grounds for demurrer; the only remedy of the defendant is a motion to add parties who

27. Sec. 32, now MASS. GEN. L. (1920), c. 231, § 136.

28. Murphy v. Russell, 202 Mass. 480, 89 N. E. 107 (1909); SCOTT, CAS. CIV. PROC. 517.

29. DICEY, PARTIES, chap. 34.

30. POMEROY, CODE REMEDIES (4 ed.), § 123; SCOTT, CAS. CIV. PROC. 206-207. Similarly the objections of want of capacity to sue, prior action pending, and misjoinder of causes of action are waived.

should have been joined, and to strike out parties who should not have been joined.[31]

The most obvious method of avoiding the effect of a mistake in a pleading is by amending the pleading. The matter of allowing amendments is as a rule within the sound discretion of the trial court. In the earlier days, the days of the maturity of the system of common-law pleading, the days of Saunders' Reports, the days when the fear of dishonoring the law by making it no art was greater than the desire to determine and enforce with reasonable speed the substantive rights of the parties, it was obviously unsportsmanlike for the courts to snatch from a party who had won a victory as a result of a slip made by his opponent in pleading, the fruits of that victory, by allowing an amendment of the defective pleading. As time has gone on, however, the courts have become increasingly liberal in the allowance of amendments, as a result of a change of view of the judges as to the end and purpose of the law of procedure, and as a result of modern statutes.[32]

31. R. S. C. (1883), Order 16, rule 11; NEW JERSEY PRACTICE ACT (1912), § 9; NEW YORK CIVIL PRACTICE ACT, § 192, Rule of Civil Practice, 102.

32. The Codes usually provide that the court may in furtherance of justice and on such terms as may be proper permit amendments at any stage of the proceedings; usually with the qualification, however, that the cause of action or defence shall not be substantially changed. There is usually also a provision directing the court to disregard errors or defects not affecting the substantial rights of the parties. See POMEROY, CODE REMEDIES. (4 ed.), § 329; SCOTT, CAS. CIV. PROC. 269.

At any time before trial, unless the party asking leave to amend is obviously seeking only to delay the proceedings, he is usually given such leave as a matter of course. When, however, by the allowance of the amendment the opposite party would be put in a worse position than that in which he would have been placed if the amended pleading had been filed in the first place, the amendment will not be allowed. Thus the defendant will not be allowed to amend his plea by alleging facts showing the liability of a third party, if the Statute of Limitations has run since the filing of the original plea, and has barred the plaintiff from recovering from the third party.[33]

At common law an amendment of the plaintiff's declaration was not allowable, if it resulted in a change in the form of action. When actions were begun by an original writ issuing not out of the court in which the action was brought, but out of Chancery, the court had no authority to hear and determine any action not within the scope of the writ. If the court was authorized by the writ to determine a cause of action in trespass, it could not thereunder determine a cause of action sounding in case. It was so held even though the parties agreed to waive the objection.[34] After original writs were abolished, and the reason for the rule had ceased, the English courts held (until forms

33. Steward v. North Metropolitan Tramways Co., 16 Q. B. D. (C. A.) 556 (1886).

34. CHITTY, PLEADING (16 Am. ed.), 109, 220.

of action were finally abolished under the Judicature Act) that an amendment changing the form of action was permissible in the discretion of the court.[35] In the United States where the system of original writs was not introduced, it was nevertheless generally held that an amendment changing the form of action is not permissible.[36] The Supreme Court of New Hampshire, however, under the leadership of Chief Justice Doe, took a broader view and held that such an amendment is permissible.[37]

In the Code states the forms of action have been abolished. It would seem therefore that in those states the rule forbidding amendments changing the form of action ought to have disappeared altogether. Unfortunately, however, this rule was replaced by one which is even worse. It was held that an amendment could not be allowed if it changed the cause of action.[38] This is in many ways a more sweeping limitation upon the power of the court than the common-law rule. Several states have by statute recently repudiated it.[39] In

35. CHITTY, PLEADING (16 Am. ed.), 220.

36. Knight v. Trim, 89 Me. 469, 36 Atl. 912 (1897); 1 ENCYC. PL. & PR. 574.

37. Stebbins v. Lancashire Ins. Co., 59 N. H. 143 (1879); Merrill v. Perkins, 59 N. H. 343 (1879); SCOTT, CAS. CIV. PROC. 261. The same result has been reached in some other states. See 3 WHITTIER, CAS. COM. L. PLEADING, 591 note.

38. Klipstein v. Raschein, 117 Wis. 248, 94 N. W. 63 (1903); SCOTT, CAS. CIV. PROC. 260. See 1 ENCYC. PL. & PR. 547; 63 U. PA. L. REV. 61.

39. N. J. LAWS, 1912, c. 231, § 24; SCOTT, CAS. CIV. PROC. 270;

some jurisdictions indeed an action at law may be amended into a suit in equity, and *vice versa*.[40] It seems clear that nothing is gained by dismissing the action and driving the plaintiff to bring a new action, when it is possible without injustice to anyone to determine the controversy by further proceedings in the original action.[41]

An amendment may be desired not only to cure a defect in the pleadings, but also to make the pleadings conform to the evidence offered or to be offered at the trial, so as to avoid a nonsuit or directed verdict for a variance. At common law no amendment could be allowed except by the full bench of the court sitting at Westminster; the judges on circuit were authorized only to try the issues raised by the pleadings, not to alter the

WIS. STATS., § 2836b (Laws 1915, c. 219, § 12). See Budding v. Murdoch, 1 Ch. D. 42 (1875) ; SCOTT, CAS. CIV. PROC. 259.

40. FEDERAL JUDICIAL CODE, § 274a; Federal Equity Rule 22; MASS. GEN. L. (1920), c. 231, § 55; WIS. STATS. 2836b (Laws 1915, c. 219, § 12). See Friederichsen v. Renard, 247 U. S. 207, 62 L. ed. 1074, 38 Sup. Ct. 450 (1918) ; Jilek v. Zahl, 162 Wis. 157, 155 N. W. 909 (1916).

In Jilek v. Zahl, *supra*, Winslow, C. J., speaking of the Wisconsin statute above cited, said: ''The beneficient effect of this provision can hardly be overestimated. It means that it will no longer be necessary to kick the plaintiff out of the back door of the courtroom (with costs) in order that he may re-enter by the front door in a different garb.''

41. If by amendment a new cause of action is substituted or added, upon which the Statute of Limitations has run at the time the amendment is made, although the statute had not run when the original action was brought, such cause of action will be barred by the statute. SCOTT, CAS. CIV. PROC. 263-266; 33 HARV. L. REV. 242.

pleadings. This rule led to so many nonsuits for slight discrepancies between the pleadings and the evidence, that Parliament finally interposed and provided that the judges at *nisi prius* should have authority to allow pleadings to be amended at the trial when a variance appeared "not material to the merits of the case, and by which the opposite party cannot have been prejudiced in the conduct of his action, prosecution or defence . . . on such terms as to payment of costs to the other party, or postponing the trial to be had before the same or another jury . . . as such court or judge shall think reasonable."[42] In the United States, either at common law or by statute, the judge at the trial may allow amendments of the pleadings, either to cure defects in the pleadings or to make them conform to the evidence.[43] If the allowing of an amendment does not operate as a surprise to the opposite party, depriving him of a fair opportunity to meet his opponent's case as amended, he is not prejudiced thereby; and of course he cannot successfully maintain that he has been deprived of property without due process of law.[44]

Greater difficulties appear when leave to amend

42. STAT. 3 & 4 WILL. IV, c. 42, § 23 (1833); SCOTT, CAS. CIV. PROC. 321.

43. N. Y. CIVIL PRACTICE ACT, § 434, formerly C. C. P., § 539; SCOTT, CAS. CIV. PROC. 322; POMEROY, CODE REMEDIES (4 ed.), § 329.

44. Seaboard Air Line Ry. v. Koennecke, 239 U. S. 352, 60 L. ed. 324, 36 Sup. Ct. 126 (1915).

is sought after the trial. If the plaintiff's declaration or complaint fails to state one of the facts necessary to constitute his cause of action, a verdict will not cure the defect, and the judgment may be arrested by the trial court on motion of the defendant, or if rendered may be reversed by an appellate court on writ of error.[45] How far is it possible by amendment after the trial to avoid the effect of the omission in the pleading? It would seem that if at the trial the omitted matter was admitted or proved by undisputed evidence, an amendment should be allowed either by the trial court or by the appellate court, and the judgment should not be arrested or reversed.[46] Thus if in an action for death by wrongful act, the plaintiff suing as administrator of the deceased failed in his complaint to make the necessary allegation that the deceased left next of kin, but at the trial offered evidence which was not contradicted showing the existence of such next of kin, and a verdict was rendered for the plaintiff, the plaintiff will be allowed to amend his complaint, and judgment for the plaintiff will not be arrested or reversed.[47] The same result is reached where there was conflicting evidence on the matter which the

45. See note 22, *supra*.

46. Slaughter v. Goldberg, Bowen & Co., 26 Cal. App. 318, 147 Pac. 90 (1915); Canavan v. Canavan, 17 N. M. 503, 131 Pac. 493 (1913) (omission of jurisdictional allegation as to residence of plaintiff in suit for divorce); Sweeney v. City of New York, 225 N. Y. 271, 122 N. E. 243 (1919).

47. Slaughter v. Goldberg, Bowen & Co., 26 Cal. App. 318, 147 Pac. 90 (1915); 3 CAL. L. REV. 339. See 50 NAT. CORP. REP. 346.

plaintiff omitted to allege, provided the matter was left to the jury for its determination.[48]

Similarly if the declaration was not defective, but the evidence offered by the plaintiff without objection did not conform to the declaration, and the matter was left to the jury, an amendment may thereafter be allowed by the trial court or by the appellate court to make the declaration conform to the evidence; or indeed the variance may be disregarded without requiring the formality of an amendment.[49] So if the defendant's plea omitted an essential allegation, but evidence was offered on the omitted matter and submitted to the jury, the plea may be amended even after verdict by the trial court or by the appellate court; or if the evidence offered did not conform to the allegations in the plea, the plea may be amended or the variance disregarded.[50]

Suppose, however, that an essential allegation is omitted from the plaintiff's declaration or complaint, and that no evidence is offered at the trial

48. Chaffee v. Rutland R. R. Co., 71 Vt. 384, 45 Atl. 750 (1899); SCOTT, CAS. CIV. PROC. 498.

49. DEC. DIG., Appeal & Error, §§ 888(2), 889.

50. In Titus v. Pennsylvania R. R. Co., 87 N. J. L. 157, 92 Atl. 944 (1915), it was suggested that if the plaintiff's evidence tends to show a defence (e. g. contributory negligence) not pleaded by the defendant because he did not know of it, the question should be left to the jury, under the liberal rules of procedure adopted by the New Jersey Practice Act, 1912. If the plaintiff's evidence clearly showed a defence though not pleaded by the defendant, the plaintiff may be nonsuited. Clark v. Oregon, etc. R. R. Co., 20 Utah, 401, 59 Pac. 92 (1899); SCOTT, CAS. CIV. PROC. 330.

as to the omitted matter. It is clear that the plaintiff is not entitled to judgment on the verdict without more. The trial court may arrest the judgment or give judgment for the defendant; or if the trial court should give judgment for the plaintiff, the appellate court may reverse the judgment and order that judgment be entered for the defendant. In that event the particular action is terminated, although the plaintiff may begin a new action, since there is no decision upon the merits. But is it necessary to drive the plaintiff to bring a new action? It would seem more reasonable to allow the plaintiff to amend his declaration by alleging the missing matter, and to grant a new trial.[51] Such a disposition of the case makes it unnecessary to start the action anew, and effects some saving of time and money. But in order to salvage as much as possible, the new trial should be confined to the matter added by the amendment. At common law partial new trials, as has been stated,[52] were not generally allowed;[53] but today they are permitted in many jurisdictions.[54]

Suppose, however, that the omitted matter is something which can be proved beyond dispute.

51. Chandler v. Chicago & Alton R. R. Co., 251 Mo. 592, 158 S. W. 35 (1913).

52. See 33 HARV. L. REV. 249. See also Chapter IV, note 10, *supra*.

53. See Chandler v. Chicago & Alton R. R. Co., 251 Mo. 592, 158 S. W. 35 (1913).

54. See Chapter IV, notes 13 & 14, *supra*.

In such a case it ought to be possible for the trial court or even for the appellate court to allow an amendment supplying the missing allegation, and then to receive evidence, and if the allegation is proved beyond dispute, to render or affirm judgment for the plaintiff. Similarly if the pleadings are sufficient, but no evidence is offered to prove one of the essential allegations, it should be possible for the trial court or for the appellate court to receive such incontrovertible evidence. This does not deprive the defendant of the right to trial by jury, because there is no disputable question of fact not tried by a jury.[55]

In the Report of the Special Committee to Suggest Remedies and Formulate Proposed Laws to Prevent Delay and Unnecessary Cost in Litigation, which was submitted to the American Bar Association in 1910, it is said:

> "Any court to which the cause is taken on appeal should have power to take additional evidence, by affidavit, deposition or reference to a master, for the purpose of sustaining a verdict or judgment whenever the error complained of is lack of proof of some matter capable of proof by record or other incontrovertible evidence, defective certification or failure to lay the proper foundation for evidence which can, in fact, without involving

55. See Chapter III, p. 104, *supra*.

11

some question for a jury, be shown to be competent.''[56]

The value of a practice allowing courts to take additional evidence on appeal on a matter as to which there is no real dispute, is shown in the following cases:

In *Varner* v. *Interstate Exchange*,[57] the plaintiff brought an action in Iowa, alleging that the defendant had represented that it owned a certain piece of land in Missouri, whereas in fact the land had been sold to a third party on foreclosure of a mortgage thereon. The defendant denied these allegations. At the trial the plaintiff offered in evidence a deed purporting to transfer the land under a power of sale contained in the mortgage. Verdict and judgment were given for the plaintiff. On appeal the Supreme Court of Iowa held that since no evidence had been offered to prove that such a transfer was valid under the law of Missouri, and since in Iowa a mortgage can be foreclosed only by suit in equity, the law of Missouri would be presumed to be the same; and accordingly reversed the judgment and remanded the case for a new trial. The whole case had to be tried anew, because of the failure to prove a matter which could have been proved beyond controversy by the production of a duly authenticated copy of the Missouri statute-book.[58] Even more

56. Rep. A. B. A., 1910, 645; *ibid*, 1909, 598.
57. 138 Iowa, 201, 115 N. W. 1111 (1908).
58. IOWA CODE, § 4651.

striking is the case of *Laub* v. *De Vault*.[59] In an action brought in Illinois, a copy of the General Statutes of Kansas, 1901, was offered in evidence at the trial. The appellate court held that a new trial must be ordered, because it had not been shown at the trial that the book was published under the authority of the state.

Similarly in *Chandler* v. *Chicago & Alton Railroad Company*,[60] the plaintiff brought an action against the defendant railroad for negligently causing the death of her husband. Under the statute such an action had to be brought within six months of the death. The plaintiff's petition showed that her action was brought more than nine months after the death of her husband. No objection was made to the sufficiency of the petition, however, and the plaintiff obtained a verdict and judgment. On appeal to the Supreme Court, the plaintiff asked leave to amend her petition by inserting an allegation that she had previously brought an action within six months after the death of her husband, that she was nonsuited, and that she began the present action within a year after the termination of the previous action, as permitted by statute. The court said that to allow the amendment and affirm the judgment for the plaintiff would be a "startling innovation"

59. 139 Ill. App. 398 (1908).
60. 251 Mo. 592, 158 S. W. 35 (1913).

and a "dangerous novelty," and remanded the cause for a new trial of the whole case.[61]

In a number of jurisdictions, in order to obviate the necessity of new trials in such cases as these, statutes have been passed allowing the taking of evidence on appeal.[62] The New Jersey Practice

61. The court refused to grant a partial new trial because "it would result in awkward situations and complications not conducive to the orderly administration of justice."

62. R. S. C. (1883), Order 58, rule 4; KANSAS, CODE OF CIVIL PROCEDURE, § 580; NEW JERSEY PRACTICE ACT, 1912, § 28; NEW BRUNSWICK JUD. ACT, 1909, Order 58, rule 4; NOVA SCOTIA JUD. ACT, 1920, Order 57, rule 5; MASS. GEN. L., c. 231, § 125. See Pound, "Some Principles of Procedural Reform," 4 Ill. L. Rev. 505.

In Ritchie v. Putnam, 13 Wend. (N. Y.) 524 (1835), on motion by the defendant for a new trial on the ground of the alienage of the plaintiff's father, the plaintiff was allowed to produce an exemplification of a court record showing an order admitting the plaintiff's father a citizen of the United States.

In describing the practice in the province of Ontario, Mr. Justice Riddell has said:

"Amendments of pleadings are allowed almost as of course at any stage even in the Appellate Division. Our rules in that regard are imperative not permissive—'shall' not 'may' . . .

"These amendments may be made in the proceedings before trial, they may be made at the trial, they may be made in the Appellate Division. Over and over again, in the Appellate Division in which I have the honor to sit, the objection has been taken, 'The judgment does not follow the pleadings,' and the answer made: 'Very well; we will amend the pleadings to agree with the facts.' There may be other facts which would require to be proved under the amended pleadings or other evidence which a party might desire to adduce. If so, we call the witnesses before us in the Appellate Division, and have them examined there; or sometimes facts are allowed to be proved on affidavit.

"If the facts are all before the court, we have little care for the pleadings and we care nothing for the 'state of the record.'

Act, 1912, has employed the phraseology of the committee of the American Bar Association, already referred to. The Kansas Code provides that "In all cases except those triable by a jury as a matter of constitutional right, the Supreme Court may receive further testimony, allow amendments of pleadings or process, and adopt any procedure not inconsistent with this act which it may deem necessary or expedient for a full and final hearing and determination of the cause." In pursuance of this provision, it has been held that where at the trial no evidence was offered as to the law of another state, but a decision of the highest court of that state was produced in the Supreme Court, the Supreme Court would not send the case back for a new trial.[63] The court said:

> "It would be a futile proceeding to send a cause back to the district court to investigate a question concerning which there can be no actual controversy whatever."

It is gradually coming to be seen that the pro-

. . . We care so little about the record that, in a great many cases, the amendments which are ordered to be made are not made in fact." 5 Amer. Bar. Ass'n Jour. 646, 647 (1919).

63. Robinson v. Chicago Ry. Co., 96 Kans. 137, 150 Pac. 636 (1915).

Under the constitutional provisions guaranteeing the right to trial by jury, the court may not determine a question of fact as to which there is a real dispute. Hess v. Conway, 93 Kans. 246, 144 Pac. 205 (1914). *Cf. Re* Fraser, 26 Ont. L. R. 508, 8 D. L. R. 955 (1912).

cedural law does not exist as an end in itself, but as a means of determining and enforcing with reasonable speed and at reasonable cost the substantive right of the parties. Except in so far as the rules of procedure are conducive to the accomplishment of this purpose they are without justification. To accomplish this purpose it is necessary indeed to require a certain amount of orderliness and regularity in the proceedings. To compel the parties to proceed in an orderly way, violations of the rules may be penalized. But the punishment should fit the crime. It is unfair to throw a case out of court because of a mistake made by one party which has in no way injured his opponent. It is unfair to compel a new trial of the whole case for a mistake affecting only a separable part of the case. It is unfair to compel a new trial of any part of the case for a mistake which, without affecting the rights of the parties, can be cured without a new trial.

The commissioners who were appointed in Massachusetts in the middle of the last century to revise and reform the proceedings in the courts of justice of that commonwealth, went to the heart of the matter when they said:

> "It was found that it [common-law pleading] had great defects as a practical system. In perfectly skillful and cautious hands it worked admirably, but, unfortunately, perfect knowledge of so complicated and subtle a system, and extreme vigilance in the use of

it, are things not to be reckoned on in practice; and accordingly this sharp and powerful
machine inflicted many wounds on the ignorant and unwary.''

The courts therefore should have a wide discretion in allowing amendments, either before the
trial, at the trial or after the trial. All that a
litigant should be allowed to insist upon is an
opportunity to present his own case, and fair
notice of and an opportunity to meet his opponent's case; and, where he is entitled to trial by
jury, to have a jury determine disputable questions of fact raised by the pleadings.

INDEX

www.ingramcontent.com/pod-product-compliance
Lightning Source LLC
Chambersburg PA
CBHW021558210326
41599CB00010B/502